Guide to
Housing
Alternatives
for Olde
Citizens

Consumer Reports Books

Guide to Housing Alternatives for Older Citizens

Margaret Gold, Ph. D.

Consumer Reports Books

To my parents, Matthew and Evelyn Klein,
and to the memory of Frank Samuel Gold.

CONSUMER REPORTS BOOKS GUIDE TO HOUSING ALTERNATIVES
FOR OLDER CITIZENS is a Consumer Reports Book published by Consumers
Union, the nonprofit organization that publishes *Consumer Reports,* the
monthly magazine of test reports, product Ratings, and buying guidance.
Established in 1936, Consumers Union is chartered under the Not-For-Profit
Corporation Law of the State of New York.

The purposes of Consumers Union, as stated in its charter, are to provide
consumers with information and counsel on consumer goods and services, to
give information on all matters relating to the expenditure of the family income,
and to initiate and to cooperate with individual and group efforts seeking to
create and maintain decent living standards.

Consumers Union derives its income solely from the sale of *Consumer
Reports* and other publications. In addition, expenses of occasional public
service efforts may be met, in part, by nonrestrictive, noncommercial
contributions, grants, and fees. Consumers Union accepts no advertising or
product samples and is not beholden in any way to any commercial interest. Its
Ratings and reports are solely for the use of the readers of its publications.
Neither the Ratings nor the reports may be used in advertising or for any
commercial purpose. Consumers Union will take all steps open to it to prevent
such uses of its material, its name, or the name of *Consumer Reports.*

Preparation of the *Consumer Reports Books Guide to Housing Alternatives for
Older Citizens* was supported by the U.S. Administration of Aging, the U.S.
Department of Housing and Urban Development, and the Florence V. Burden
Foundation. The statements and conclusions contained herein are those of the
author and do not necessarily reflect the views of the U.S. Government in
general or HUD or AoA in particular.

Contents

Acknowledgments

M any individuals and organizations contributed significantly to the *Consumer Reports Books Guide to Housing Alternatives for Older Citizens*. The Institute for Consumer Policy Research, a department of Consumers Union, sponsored the work, and preparation was supported by grants from the Florence V. Burden Foundation, the U.S. Administration on Aging, and the U.S. Department of Housing and Urban Development.

I am indebted to a great many people who freely contributed their time and expertise. Special thanks are due David Nee of the Burden Foundation and Debbie Greenstein of HUD for their generous and painstaking reviews of entire drafts of the manuscript.

Pamela Booth (National HomeCaring Council), Dennis Day-Lower and Leah Dobkin (Shared Housing Resource Center), Leo Baldwin (American Association of Retired Persons), Patrick Hare, Dr. Mark Olshan (B'Nai B'Rith), Virginia Robinson, (Action for Boston Community Development), and Henry Whitlock (Federal Trade Commission) each reviewed individual chapters or sections related to their field of knowledge. Their contributions have been invaluable.

I am grateful to Jean Halloran, Director of the Institute for Consumer Policy Research, for her insightful comments, her excellent editorial work, and her vision of the Guide's potential. Joyce Newman of Consumers Union contributed steadfast personal and professional support during difficult periods. Catherine Bradshaw and Jean Marie Andresen provided research assistance at crucial junctures. Greg Williamson's word-processing virtuosity and his patience throughout many revisions will be remembered.

—MARGARET GOLD, PH.D.

Guide to Housing Alternatives for Older Citizens

Introduction

The idea for this book developed from a number of conversations with older people and their families. Some were people we knew personally—friends, relatives and the relatives of friends. Some were people we interviewed professionally about events having little to do with housing. Often, though, the interviews settled upon a subject that was on many people's minds—where and how to spend the years ahead.

Many of the people we spoke to had recently experienced significant life changes, such as widowhood, increasing health limitations, and having to live on a set income. For others, impending retirement was raising many questions. Many looked forward to what they could do once they were free from the obligations imposed by earning a living and raising children. However, few people believed that their physical and financial capacities would be unaffected by time. Some people in midlife were less concerned about their own future than they were about the situation of aging parents. Nevertheless, money and physical energy were assets that had to be carefully considered and rationed as *both* generations set about planning for the future.

If you, too, have been giving serious thought to your future or are presently concerned with your parents' welfare, taking a look at the broader picture can provide some perspective.

Today twenty-eight million Americans are 65 years or older—about 11 percent of the total population. The proportion of over-65s to other age groups has been steadily increasing since the turn of the century. It is expected to peak in the year 2030, when sixty-seven million people—over 20 percent of all Americans—will be 65 or older.

Where, with whom, and how are older Americans currently living? The popular image of older people clustered closely together in the Sunbelt is mostly myth. It *is* true that Florida, with 17.5 percent of residents over age 65, is home to a large population of older adults. No other state comes close to having such a large share of over-65 residents. Of the twenty U.S. cities with the largest concentrations of older people, sixteen are in Florida and some fifteen thousand new residents over 65 reportedly arrive in the state each month.

Regardless of the numbers, most of the nation's older people do *not* live in warm climates. Almost half the nation's older population lives in seven states—New York, Illinois, California, Ohio, Pennsylvania, Texas, and Florida—only three of which are in or near the Sunbelt. For sheer numbers, New York City, with almost a million older adults, outpaces all other American cities. Its over-65 population is triple that of the nearest contenders, Chicago and Los Angeles.

Obviously, many older people are choosing to stay exactly where they are—in the cities and states where they were born, worked, and raised families. They are also, it would seem, pioneering new living arrangements geared both to their larger numbers and to changing circumstances.

In many cases, this requires a fair amount of creativity. Older people, as a group, are actually better off than in the past, but many are managing on lower incomes. The average income of a couple over 65 is $12,965. The median for a single man is $8,200; for a single woman it is only $4,800.

For many, paying off the mortgage has brought some financial relief. Of the 28 million older people in the United States, 17 million are head of households who own houses. Of these, 13 million own their houses mortgage-free. Some of these paid-for houses can be a mixed blessing, though. Over half were built before 1950. Partly because they require constant maintenance, partly because of older people's smaller incomes, elderly people on the average, spend 34% of their income on housing—a higher figure than the general population.

The fact is that most older people do live independently in their own households, either alone or with a spouse. Some 30 percent—most of them women—live alone, with the percentage growing as age increases. Contrary to many people's image of the old, only 5 percent of those over 65 reside in a nursing home, although the figure increases to 20 percent of those over 85. Some 18 percent of older people live with children or other relatives; this percentage also rises with age.

As we talked with older people, it became clear that very few *wanted* to live with their children as a solution to health or financial problems. Reluctance to enter a nursing home was even stronger. Yet many people were resigned to these two alternatives as the only ones available to themselves or loved ones once they could no longer manage on their own.

Perhaps you, too, are not aware of too many other options. Even if you have been thinking about possible alternative arrangements, you may have already discovered that getting reliable up-to-date information on which to base your planning is not easy. Chances are, the facts available have come to you in somewhat random fashion. Perhaps you've seen newspaper or TV ads for retirement communities or for home health care—two commodities heavily marketed to older people these days. How much can you trust the advertiser's statements? Are there other, less publicized alternatives you might like better? If so, how can you discover these alternatives and compare them?

You or your parents may also have heard or read about low-cost government-subsidized apartments for older people, but the idea of involvement with a large bureaucracy is discouraging. Just finding the right agency to call for information, out of dozens with alphabet-soup titles, can be discouraging. Besides, you may have heard that low-cost senior apartments have such long waiting lists that applying for them is futile.

Stories about older people sharing their homes with one or more housemates are appearing in the popular media more and more. These stories make home sharing sound like an attractive, sensible solution to many people's housing problems. But home sharing is not for everyone. How can you tell if it would work for you or members of your family? Living with another person is sometimes difficult. Some people feel it is risky even to let a stranger in their home to discuss the possibility of sharing. Some media stories describe match-up programs that bring compatible housemates together, and help them reach a reasonable agreement. But you've never heard of such a program in your area. What can you do?

If you decide to create an information file about housing and living options either for yourself or together with an older relative who may be considering a move, your task will not be easy, because information on this subject is scattered through many sources. And much of it is biased because it is furnished by commercial interests in the field.

This book is designed to meet such information needs, with each chapter describing one or more major type of housing option. Of course, no single book could possibly cover every innovation in living that has been devised; we present those options that are most generally available nationwide. In addition, we include a few that are not in wide use at present but are worth noting because they are sensible.

We begin with the question of whether to make a household move at all. If you are inclined to stay put but are worried that you may *have* to move, you certainly want to make sure you are exploiting all available options that could help you remain where you are. These include financial remedies for homeowners and renters as well as supportive, health-related services available inside and outside your home. And then there is home sharing, an option many people are now investigating seriously.

The succeeding chapters are devoted to living arrangements that will most likely involve relocating. Here are the housing options you will find described in the chapters ahead. Some of the terms are new and unfamiliar—*they will become clearer as you read along.*

Accessory apartments. These are created by installing a completely separate living unit in what was originally a one-family dwelling. Often called "in-law suites," accessory apartments are multiplying rapidly in suburban communities across the country, housing perhaps 1.5 million older Americans.

Echo housing. Also called elder housing or "granny flats," these are detached, removable units placed on the same lot with a one-family or multiple-family house. Intended for rural and suburban communities, only a few of these new units have actually been installed so far.

Small group residences are small apartment buildings or large houses in which from four to forty people reside and share daily responsibilities. They are usually sponsored by nonprofit community agencies, but some are simply independent rooming houses for older people. No one knows how many of these presently exist, although the numbers are large.

Senior apartments. This is a catchall term. It applies mainly to low-cost apartment dwellings subsidized by federal, state or local agencies or by private, not-for-profit sponsors. A specified package of health and social services is sometimes included along with the housing. The U.S. Department of Housing and Urban Development has built 170,000 such units.

Retirement communities are privately developed, generally more expensive homes or apartment complexes, offering the maximum in service, recreation and "easy living." Retirement communities range in size from a single building to whole "villages" or "towns." The best-known, and largest, Sun City in Arizona, houses thirty thousand people.

Life care or continuing care are terms that describe a special type of retirement community. In return for a sizeable entrance fee, residents are guaranteed a permanent place to live and a specified package of medical and nursing care. A recent innovation, continuing-care communities carry significant financial risks that require serious study by consumers. There are perhaps five hundred life-care facilities nationwide as of 1985, but their numbers are growing.

Adult foster homes are private homes in which small groups of partly disabled adults are cared for.

Nursing facilities. In spite of their negative image, nursing homes are not all alike! Basically, nursing facilities are designed to offer three kinds of care: skilled nursing, intermediary nursing (for the less disabled) and custodial care (for people who aren't seriously ill but can no longer maintain daily housekeeping and personal chores). As we noted before, fewer older people than you might expect live in nursing homes—only 5 percent of the over-65 population, although 20 percent of the over-85 population.

Within each chapter, we will answer the following questions about each of the options under discussion:

1. How did this type of living arrangement get started? What kinds of people and groups have supported it?

2. What are the overall goals of this type of housing arrangement?

3. Who is eligible for this option? What health, financial, or other requirements are there?

4. What are the typical physical and architectural features of this form of housing?

5. What are present and future financial costs likely to be?

6. What kinds of services are included in the housing package?

7. What are the possibilities for companionship and social life?

8. What will your relationship with sponsors and managers be like? Who makes the rules and decisions?

9. How does this form of housing relate to the surrounding community? How receptive is the neighborhood to residents?

10. How can you find out more about this type of living arrangement? (Questions to ask, what to look for when visiting, negotiating a contract, when to get professional help.)

At the end of each chapter, we list a few key resources that can provide you with more detailed information about the type of housing arrangements described in the chapter. The Appendix provides fuller listings including all State Offices or Departments of Aging and many other organizations concerned with benefiting older Americans, and with housing in particular.

There is no correct way to read and use this book. You may feel like reading it from cover to cover. Or you may want to start with a housing option that interests you and then read about other areas at your leisure. Some experts in the field suggest filling out financial and health checklists before investigating specific living arrangements they believe will be of assistance in analyzing your situation as you read about the various housing options available to you, and we have provided these in Chapter One and in the Appendix.

Chapter 1

Starting Out

This guide is offered as a single, comprehensive, reliable information source on the subject of housing and living arrangements for older people. You can turn to it for descriptions of a wide range of options and alternatives and weigh the advantages and disadvantages of those options, matching them with your own personal circumstances. Finally, it will help you develop consumer skills in shopping for and negotiating the best possible living arrangement. It specifies what questions to ask, when to ask them and how to organize the answers you receive.

Everyone is welcome to use this book, but it is meant primarily for three groups of people: those contemplating retirement, those who are already retired or just approaching what are euphemistically called "the golden years," and those older people considering the possibility of making a change in their present living arrangements.

If you share your parents' or another older relative's concerns about the future, this book is for you as well. While learning about your parents' options, you will be laying a foundation that will serve you well also when planning for your own later life.

This book can also be useful to professionals who work with older people and their families. Information in this field is diffuse, and a central information source on housing options can save time and assure that you haven't overlooked an alternative that could suit your client or patient. The materials presented here are also adaptable for use in community education efforts, such as workshops, pre-

and post-retirement seminars and support groups for adult children who are taking a responsible role in the lives of their aging parents.

Will Moving Be Bad for Your Health?

The living arrangements to be discussed in the next chapters will often involve a household move. Can a move, in itself, be dangerous? A great many studies have been made about the effects of a late-life move on older people. As most of us already know from experience, a move at any age involves considerable disruption. Studies of relocation and older people have traditionally been concerned with effects of moving on health, mental well-being and longevity. These studies don't always agree with one another, and it is risky to generalize from them.

For example, some early studies showed that frail, chronically ill older people who were moved from their homes to some type of institution tended to weaken and die sooner than others who were not moved. This reinforced the popular notion that moving, like retirement, was essentially bad for older people and should be avoided.

Later studies revealed that moving, per se, was not necessarily the cause of the health problems experienced by the original group. If the move was to a homelike rather than an institutional setting, if it brought increased social stimulation to a previously isolated person and did not entail the loss of important attachments, a move could help rather than harm. For many people, a retirement move, perhaps to a Sunbelt leisure community, can be the realization of a dream—a long-awaited opportunity to escape cold winters and enjoy beaches and golf courses year round.

One researcher into the effects of relocation stresses that two important factors affect your reaction to a late-life move: whether or not you choose the move and whether or not it brings about a significantly improved living situation. Still other experts emphasize the importance of keeping social contacts alive if a move is to be carried out without more than temporary ill-effects. You may not wish actually to live with relatives or friends, but if they occupy a very important place in your daily life, having them within your geographical area should be a top consideration in your planning.

To make good choices among the housing arrangements reviewed here, it is extremely important to establish your priorities.

A Priority Exercise

A good way to begin thinking about where and how to live in the future is to make some checklists. This system enables you to focus on the specifics of your situation while you're still collecting and sorting out information. Often, checklists and inventories can also help you screen out unsuitable options right from the start.

We suggest you begin by doing a simple priority exercise right now. If you are thinking about a change in living arrangements together with an older relative or your parents, ask them if they-would like to do this exercise. It will be a quick way to summarize the individual needs and preferences that shape decisions about living arrangements and the rest of the book will become more meaningful and helpful.

To begin, take a sheet of ruled paper and list the following items on the left hand side, one under the other, double spaced.

- Climate

- Neighborhood safety

- Visual appearance of neighborhood

- House or apartment security

- Visual appearance and state of repair of exterior

- Visual appearance and state of repair of interior

- Structural features (elevators, ramps, handrails)

- Cost (rent or mortgage payment)

- Access to public transportation

- Proximity to medical care

- Proximity to shopping

- Proximity to church or recreation center

- Daily presence of another person in the home or very close by

- Assistance with heavy cleaning and housekeeping

- Assistance with light housekeeping

- Assistance with personal chores (bathing, laundry, shopping, cooking)

- Privacy

- Proximity to family (close enough to visit weekly)

- Proximity to friends (close enough to visit weekly)

- Neighborliness

Add to these, whenever they arise, any other features of housing and living that are important to you.

Now, put a plus sign next to each item about which you feel generally satisfied or which you feel is not an important consideration. Answer in terms of how you feel today—don't try to anticipate the future. Place a minus sign next to those items with which you're presently dissatisfied or that you feel are significant problems. (If you're undecided, leave a blank or indicate a question mark and return to that one later.)

Next, go down the list of items once again. Rate each item according to how important it is in your life right now. Use a "1" for high priorities, a "2" for ones that are secondary and a "3" for items that have low priority for you.

Take a good look at all the "1" scores that have pluses next to them. Obviously, these are the things you value most about your present living situation. For the short term, at least, you shouldn't sacrifice or compromise these items any more than you absolutely have to.

Look closely now at "1" scores that are accompanied by minuses. They contain the picture of just what would have to change, if you are to be happier with your living arrangements. You may want to put these changes in rank order, with the most important ones first, if you are clear in your own mind about that.

Another thing you can do is to list your one pluses and one minuses under two headings, called Keep and Change. If you have a large number of keeps and hardly any changes, that tells you something. (Of course, it may still be very important to you to make those few changes, especially if economy is one of them.) If the reverse is true and you have a large proportion of changes, you know you need to look for some alternatives without undue delay.

The last step in this exercise is to ask yourself, "What do I like best about my present living arrangements?" Don't reflect upon this too long. Write what comes to mind immediately. It's best to limit the list to three. Now ask yourself, "What do I like least about my living arrangements?" and answer in the same way. Your two statements don't commit you to anything—they are simply food for thought.

You can take an intermission now, or start the whole exercise over again. Only this time, you fill in the columns while imagining what life will be like in seven to ten years. True—only a prophet or magician would attempt to predict. We suggest only that you use your self-knowledge and experience to make some educated guesses about what will be important to you in the future.

Although this exercise can be very helpful, it is not a formula for successful decision-making! None of the priorities you choose are written in stone. Some may be reinforced by experience. Others may change with the passage of time. The purpose of the exercise is to help clarify, focus, and generally get a good handle on your present and future living situations.

A Financial Checklist

Just as important as what you would like, is what you can afford. Not that you should be discouraged by what may appear to be financial limitations—there are several ways to make living arrangements to live in a warm climate, if that is what you or your parents would most like to do at this time, just as there are several ways you may be unaware of to make arrangements to stay in one's own home (as we will see in Chapter Two). What is important is knowing what you have to work with, financially.

We therefore suggest that you take some time and work on the Estimated Monthly Income Chart and the Total Assets and Net Worth Chart that appear on the following pages. As you can see, the charts are largely self-explanatory. At this time, you may not want to have an antique gold necklace you inherited five years ago appraised to find out what it is worth. But it's still a good idea to make a start. In the chapters ahead, we provide a fair amount of information concerning hourly rates, monthly costs, admission fees, and down payments for various types of living arrangements. You will probably find it useful to do some preliminary work on this chart now so as to have the bottom line as a basis of comparison. Then, if you decide to consider one or another housing option seriously, and need a realistic view of your financial situation, you can come back and complete the chart with greater accuracy. Should you need any help, detailed instruction for filling out the chart appear in Chapter Six.

About Planning

These checklists are neither a formula nor a game. We hope they will serve as a preamble to active planning. Planning does take a good deal of work, but your work can make the time ahead more rewarding, more carefree, and less anxious. And that's what this book is all about.

TOTAL ASSETS AND NET WORTH CHART

Types of Assets		Dollar Amt.
(1) Savings Account—enter total amount in the savings account, not the interest it produces		$
(2) Money Market Funds, Certificates of Deposit—enter principal amount on this line		$
(3) Stocks—enter current market price, not original purchase price		$
(4) Bonds—enter face value of bonds, not interest they pay		$
(5) Real Estate—enter appraised value or market value, not original purchase price (if rented, *do not* put rent amount; that is listed on Estimated Monthly Income Chart)		$
(6) Personal Property (household goods, automobiles, furs, etc.)—enter present value, not purchase price		$
(7) Antiques, Jewels, Collectibles (stamps, coins)—enter present value, as appraised		$
(8) OTHER ASSETS		
(a)		$
(b)		$
(c)		$
(d)		$
(9) Total: Gross Value of Assets (add 1 through 8d)		$
(10) OBLIGATIONS/DEBTS/LOSS OF VALUE		
(a)	$	
(b)	$	
(c)	$	
(d)	$	
(11) Total (add 10a through 10d)	$	$
(12) Total Net Worth (subtract 11 from 9)		$

* ESTIMATED MONTHLY INCOME			
Sources of Income	Present Monthly Income	Six Months from Now	Two Years from Now
(1) Social Security—enter the amount of monthly check			
(2) Retirement/Pension (usually private retirement or government pension, such as an IRA or annuity, not social security)—enter amount received			
(3) Private Insurance (for long-term-care insurance, check benefits paid)—enter amount			
(4) Bank Accounts, Stocks, Bonds, etc.—enter the interest income these accounts generate, not the principal or face value			
(5) Debts Income—enter the monthly payment received (do not enter the amount of the debt)			
(6) Real Estate Rental Income—enter the amount of rent received per month (do not list the value of the property)			
(7) Antiques/Valuables—enter only if selling these items on a monthly basis (if not, list total value on Total Assets Chart)			
(8) Family Pledges/Contributions—enter monthly amounts received, not lump sum amounts			
(9) Medicare—if eligible, an insurance program that covers skilled nursing care for 100 days (after 21st day person contributes $38/day)			
(10) Medicaid—an entitlement program for low-income individuals; eligibility requirement will vary from state to state			
(11) Supplementary Security Income (an entitlement program that has certain eligibility requirements: monthly amounts may vary)—enter amount of monthly check			
(12) Union/Fraternal/Veteran benefits (if a member of any organization that pays sick or long-term-care benefits)—enter amount received			
(13) Gross Monthly Income (add 1 through 12)			
(14) Less Obligations/Expenses			
(15) Net Monthly Income (subtract 14 from 13)			

* See Chapter Six for detailed explanation of how to fill out chart.

Chapter 2

Staying Put

Y ou may know exactly how you want to spend the rest of your life. If you—or your family—are fortunate, you may even have the means to carry out all your plans. But, for most of us, life brings changes, sooner or later, that call for modifying our plans. Decisions about major changes, such as moving, are not usually made quickly, so you will want to sort out all your options and weigh each one carefully.

Not all reasons for a late-life move are negative ones. This may be the chance to realize a long-held wish or dream: to live near ocean or mountains, to devote serious attention to a talent or avocation, to try a type of community living ruled out earlier by work or family obligations. How closely can you approximate your dream? What are the financial and emotional costs? How permanent a commitment will this be? What if you want to make a change again?

Every move involves a tradeoff between what you have now and what you exchange it for. There is no one right way of arriving at the best tradeoff. Every thoughtful decision reflects some combination of logic and emotion, to which reliable information contributes. In this chapter, we will present information that can help you decide whether you are better off staying put or relocating.

Before deciding whether or not a move is in order, you will first want to make sure you are exploiting the current options as fully as possible. The rest of this chapter will describe steps that can be taken to adapt life in your present house or apartment to your changing needs.

Even if you feel ripe for a change, there are probably some advantages to staying put. Some of the financial options we describe in this chapter may make staying in your present home less of a financial burden than you expected. We will also discuss a variety of community resources that can help meet changing health and social needs while remaining in your present home.

And, finally, we will consider home sharing as a strategy for continuing independence that many people are turning to.

Charlotte Sharp is 71 years old. She and her husband first moved into her pleasant two-bedroom apartment in upper Manhattan twenty-five years ago. Charlotte's apartment is rent-controlled, so she doesn't worry too much about rent increases. But there are some tradeoffs. She lives on the fourth floor of her apartment building. There is no elevator. There is no buzzer to let visitors into the building's locked vestibule. She has to walk down the stairs to let someone in, and then walk up again. Carrying up groceries and laundry, she must stop to rest at each landing.

During the winter, Charlotte fell and broke several ribs. She considered going into a nursing home, but her ribs healed and she decided not to file the applications. She also considered moving in with her children in Texas, but 'her room' is presently occupied by her married grandson and his wife, both of whom are job hunting. "So that's out," she says.

She also considered Lincoln Square, an apartment building for senior citizens in a neighborhood about five miles south of her present apartment. But Charlotte has heard that the residents who live there now are being moved out. Rising real estate values in that neighborhood have made those apartments more desirable than they were when the developer first advertised them as senior citizen housing. "If there were somewhere else I could afford, I'd move," she says, looking up at the ceiling, where a little plaster is starting to peel away. Charlotte is weighing the pros and cons of moving, and looking at her options. For now, she's decided to stay put.

Financial Programs For Older Homeowners And Renters

If you would like to remain in your present home, the major obstacles may be financial ones. Inflation—especially the runaway inflation of the 1970s—has continued to affect the lives of all of us. Financial problems and solutions for homeowners and renters differ in many respects, so we'll discuss them separately.

First, the options for owners. If you are over 65, the chances are good that you own your own home and your mortgage is paid up. Three-quarters of all heads of households over age 65 own their homes. What this probably means is that your home is your single largest financial asset.

Yet regardless of no longer having to meet those monthly mortgage payments, you may still feel financially pressed. Fuel costs (which tripled between 1972 and 1983), property taxes (up 67 percent for the same period), plus increased costs of insurance, utilities, and home repairs may leave you feeling "house rich and cash poor." Many people with fixed incomes—especially those for whom social security is their sole income—live near the poverty line inside their paid-for homes. You or your adult children may have wondered more than once if there is a safe way the value of your home could be made more useful to you in the time ahead.

Home Equity Conversion Plans

Many financial analysts have pointed out that the major resource of older homeowners is their home equity. Traditionally, people with fixed incomes were advised to put their equity to work by selling their homes and investing the proceeds. Recently, some innovative ideas for unlocking this source of money without giving up your home have been tried out experimentally in a few localities. These plans are known in the field as home-equity conversion (HEC) plans.

Three different types of HEC plans have evolved from the fundamental idea that equity, converted into cash, can boost buying power and improve quality of life for many older people. The three variations are: reverse mortgage plans, sale-leaseback plans, and special deferred payment loans to upgrade or modify homes.

Reverse mortgages do work somewhat like a conventional mortgage in reverse. The lender pays you, the homeowner, a monthly amount, which is considered to be a loan against the equity in your house. You do not sell the house—the house is your collateral. You do not have to repay this loan (and the accrued interest) until the end of a term that may run anywhere from five to fifteen years. The usual expectation is that the home will eventually be sold in order to satisfy the debt fully. (Any money left over goes to you or your estate.) The most obvious problem is that you could outlive the term of the loan and risk losing your house. Some innovative programs are finding ways around this hazard. For example, a New Jersey lender has provided for deferred repayment until age 100, with homeowner and lender both sharing the home's appreciation.

In a **sale-leaseback** plan, an investor buys the home (at a price from 15 - 25 percent below the market value) and immediately leases it back to the former owner for life. The new owner assumes taxes, insurance, major repairs and other expenses usually associated with home ownership. Payment to the seller usually consists of a lump-sum down payment plus monthly payments. Rental is negotiable. A contract spells out in detail the rights and obligations of both parties. Sale-leaseback contracts also contain complicated clauses specifying, for example, what will happen in the event of the original owner's death.

Deferred-payment loans are made to a homeowner for a specific purpose, such as modernizing, repairing or weatherizing the house. They usually carry low interest rates and repayment is not due until the owner dies or the house is sold. A number of variations on deferred payment loans have been described that do not offer cash but charge off certain expenses (e.g., property taxes or home care) as a lien against the property.

Home-equity conversion plans have a great deal of potential for benefitting older homeowners. On the other hand, they are highly complex and contain potential hazards. Because they are both new and complicated, they are not thoroughly understood by many financial, legal and real estate professionals. Finding competent, impartial information and advice is not easy. Some programs in California and New Jersey offer consumer counseling through an independent, disinterested community agency. If you live elsewhere and are interested in investigating HECs, you should start by writing the National Center for Home Equity Conversion (NCHEC), an information clearinghouse and watchdog organization. The American Association of Retired Persons (AARP) can also provide you with competent, unbiased information. (See listings for both organizations at the chapter's end.)

A number of national organizations have endorsed the concept of home equity conversion, provided that appropriate consumer safeguards are implemented. Safeguards recommended by NCHEC and AARP include:

- legal and financial counseling for homeowners considering these plans;

- an insurance program to protect homeowners against loss of property due to misrepresentation and fraud or due to outliving the term of the agreement;

- strict laws and penalties for those who attempt to exploit older people through high pressure sales tactics, inadequate disclosure, fraud or deceit.

As more experience with home-equity conversion accumulates, we hope that safeguards and standards will emerge, to minimize risks and enable more older homeowners to reap the benefits these plans can offer.

Tax Relief for Owners

Other financial relief for older homeowners includes various forms of tax abatement, and, in some locales, discounted utility rates. Many states have passed some type of property tax relief for older citizens. These include the so-called "circuit breaker," which reduces property taxes according to income (the smaller the income, the smaller the tax). Circuit breakers do not exist in every state and vary with local and state tax laws. But they are too substantial to overlook, so check with your area Office on Aging or local housing department to see if your state has one and if you are eligible. To illustrate—a 1983 Illinois circuit-breaker program available to older or disabled persons gave a maximum grant of $700 (minus 5 percent of household income) plus a grant of $80 to all qualified applicants.

Some other forms of tax relief for older homeowners include homestead exemptions that reduce the assessed value of owner-occupied homes, property tax freezes, deferrals of tax payments until the owner's death or the sale of the house, and tax credits of various kinds.

Most forms of tax abatement are greatly underused. In Oregon, only 15 percent of all eligible households participate in the tax-deferral program—and that is one of the highest rates in the nation! In Washington, D.C., fewer than half the homeowners eligible for the homestead tax exemption actually apply.

Don't miss out just because you are unaware of the tax relief programs available to you. These programs are not well publicized, and you will probably have to seek them out. The best way to start is to call your nearest State Office on Aging (see Appendix D) or your local property tax office and ask to speak to someone about tax programs for homeowners. They will be able to help you make sure you are getting all the tax advantages and benefits to which you're entitled.

Options for Renters

Renters are, in some ways, a more vulnerable group than owners. This doesn't mean that all renters are disadvantaged. For some, renting is a highly satisfactory way of life. If you or your parent occupy a rent controlled apartment, you are in a very fortunate position, provided the building is kept in good repair, adequately serviced and secure.

However, you may find you are spending a third or more of your income on housing. That's not so unusual for older renters. But it exceeds the 30 percent of income considered by the federal government a "safe and reasonable" proportion to spend on housing. Although your building or neighborhood may be showing signs of deterioration, you may still feel a strong attachment to your long-time surroundings and don't really want to leave. What can you do?

Financial strategies designed for renters have been sparse, compared with those benefitting homeowners. Rent control is controversial and affects fewer and fewer units each year. But being over 65 may protect you from displacement due to condominium or co-op conversion, depending on where you live.

A few creative and innovative plans for renters have been introduced, usually on a local level. Most are aimed at enabling older people with moderate incomes to purchase units they formerly rented, particularly in urban neighborhoods that are being revitalized. The best-known plan is to sell the apartment jointly to the tenant and an outside investor—or wholly to an outside investor, who agrees to keep the rent low. This plan is referred to as "shared equity."

Like other new mortgage ideas, shared equity involves pitfalls and risks. Before participating in any such plan, be sure to investigate it with an objective party, such as a lawyer, banker, or accountant.

A final word about government programs to build and/or renovate low-cost rental apartments for older Americans: under the Department of Housing and Urban Development (HUD) "Section 202" program, direct loans are made at low interest rates to nonprofit sponsoring organizations for the building of specially designed housing for the "elderly and handicapped."

About 170,000 units have been built across the country under this program. Although proposals were made to end the program in 1985, Congress did authorize funds to build 24,000 more units in 1986 and 1987. This is a step in the right direction, but it is not enough. The size of the elderly population continues to grow. The demand heavily outweighs the supply and waiting lists are long. Further changes are expected to come about only as a result of political pressure. (More information about low-cost rental housing is contained in Chapter Four.)

HUD's Section 8 programs also are designed to improve the quality of rental-occupied housing. Some programs offer tenants direct subsidies, while others are geared toward the rehabilitation of buildings. Section 8 provisions are complicated. If you are a resident of urban lower-cost rental housing and would like more information about Section 8 programs, we suggest calling your State Office on Aging (see Appendix D) or your local housing department.

Health Services And Programs For Older People Living At Home

Many older people with limited health and energy can continue to live independently in their homes—provided the right kind of services and assistance are available.

According to the government, up to 40% of older people now in nursing homes don't really need to be there. Many would still be at home if only homemaker/home health aide and transportation services could have been extended to them in time.

It *is* true that government resources and programs of all kinds have been sharply cut over the last few years, and services for older people weren't spared. However, homemaker/home health aide services are increasingly being reimbursed by third party payers, such as Medicare and many private insurers.

The availability of health services and programs varies greatly from one locality to the next. Many communities contain a large but fragmented array of programs and agencies. If you live in such a community, your biggest problem will be to locate and coordinate the different kinds of services you may require. Other communities are sadly underserved. Their residents have to depend more heavily on family, neighbors and church for assistance.

The best solution is to become as familiar as you can with existing resources in your own community. Putting together the right combination of services may make the difference between having to relocate and being able to stay put. Once you have entered this helping network, there should be assistance in fulfilling your requirements.

Home Care Services: What Are They? Who Needs Them?

If you or an older relative are having some health problem or can't find the energy for necessary daily tasks, don't assume you have to give up your home. There are home-care services available that may allow you to stay put, if that is what you'd like to do.

Home care covers a broad range of services, offered temporarily or on a regular basis. One person might need regular assistance because of a health condition that limits his or her functioning, such as arthritis or failing vision. Another might need short-term home care while recovering from an illness or from surgery. Home care can be provided by Visiting Nurses, at a fairly typical cost of $40 per visit, which may be covered by Medicare or other insurance. Skilled-nursing care by the day (or night) is also available through the types of private and public agencies described below. Costs for skilled nurses (R.N.s or L.P.N.s) are highly variable—you may have to pay as much as $25 per hour for a registered nurse, but you may also be eligible for some insurance or Medicare coverage if the service is ordered by your doctor and follows discharge from the hospital.

Many agencies also offer full or part-time home health aide/homemaker services for assistance with personal care and household chores. Fees for home health aides run anywhere from $8 and upwards hourly. Variations in home nursing costs change from locality to locality, but fees differ within localities, too, so it pays to compare. Alternative ways of meeting nursing care costs are described in more detail later on in this chapter.

Home care can also be supplemented by other services, such as Meals on Wheels, outside home maintenance, volunteer visiting, and transportation or escort services. Sometimes it takes just a little additional service to fill in the gaps between what you need and what friends and family already provide.

Ideally, you'll want to arrange for the type and extent of home care that's best tailored to your needs. Professionals, such as hospital discharge workers attempt to match their clients' needs with available services and help clients coordinate with the appropriate agencies. But with a little consumer know-how, you or your family can probably begin the process.

One word of caution: If you or your older relative are anticipating a return home from the hospital, don't put off planning for home health care. Most third-party payments that cover these services (such as Blue Cross or Medicare) stipulate that the service must directly follow discharge from the hospital. If you wait to see how you fare on your own and then decide help is needed, chances are you won't be reimbursed. Remember, you can always discontinue assistance you no longer need!

If, during a hospital stay, you think you may need help when you get home, inform to your doctor, since he or she will have to order the service in order for coverage to take effect. If no one from the hospital's Home Care or Social Services department contacts you, then you should make an appointment to meet with them before going home. And if your hospital doesn't have such a department, ask a head nurse on your floor how you can obtain needed assistance with home care.

Who Provides Home Care?

People from a variety of occupations perform home care: registered nurses (R.N.s), licensed practical nurses (L.P.N.s), and homemaker/home health aides. Physical therapists, respiratory therapists, speech therapists, social workers, occupational therapists, and volunteers can also work with you at home. A very helpful booklet available from the National HomeCaring Council (see address at the end of the chapter) explains what each type of worker does and the level of training and skill required of each.

The type of home-care worker most in demand is the homemaker/home health aide. Homemaker/home health aides assist with personal care such as bathing, grooming, and walking. They also shop, cook, do laundry, and other light housekeeping duties.

Could this be a part-time job for you? The National HomeCaring Council says the present demand for homemaker/health aides outweighs the supply by about three to one, and the need is expected to increase dramatically over the next decade. For older women and men in good health, this could be a gratifying source of employment and income. If you are interested, address inquiries about training and employment to the National Association of Home Care, 519 C Street, NE, Washington, D.C. 20002.

You can obtain home care through three different types of agencies. It is important, in choosing and dealing with an agency, to understand which type it is and how it operates:

Employment agencies and nurses' registries will, for a fee, find and place personnel in your home. In this case, you are the employer and you pay the home-care worker directly and are responsible for social security and other employer taxes. Most such agencies take no further responsibility for supervising workers or monitoring quality of work—that is between you and the home-care worker.

Non-profit agencies (such as Visiting Nurses' Associations and Homemaker-Health Aide Services) employ personnel who are supervised and may be further trained after placement in your home. You pay the agency. The agency is responsible for the quality of its employees' work. If you have problems, you bring them to the agency, which is responsible for correcting them.

Commercial, for-profit homecare agencies are a rapidly booming industry. Because of the growing older population and the need to hold down hospital costs, these services now comprise a $2+ billion industry—a figure that is expected to at least quadruple by 1986.

Some commercial agencies are reliable, but, as the National HomeCaring Council points out, potential for abuse and fraud is present. The Council recommends following the next steps to help you avoid many pitfalls in obtaining competent services from any of the three types of agencies we've just described.

How to Find Home Care

If you think you or an older relative need some kind of home care, there are a few different ways you can begin looking for that care. Personal recommendations from friends and acquaintances can be helpful, but they are not enough. Even if you use the same agency your friend did, her worker may not be available, and the agency may send someone else.

A personal recommendation is not a substitute for becoming acquainted first-hand with the agency you deal with by asking questions about its licensing and accreditation and by requesting references. Don't be shy about asking these questions—a reputable agency does not mind answering them courteously.

Professional referrals can be another good route to quality home care. Referrals from hospital home-care departments, discharge planners, social workers, or doctors are ways of obtaining quality help, if you or an older relative are returning home from a hospital stay.

A great many people, however, find their way to good care through the telephone directory—both White and Yellow pages. The National HomeCaring Council suggests checking the phone book for such listings as:

- Information and Referral Service (I&R)
- state, county, or city agency on aging
- family service agencies (such as Catholic Charities, Jewish Family Services)
- American Red Cross, United Way, or other voluntary agency
- your local librarian
- Hot Line, Action Line, HELP, or CONTACT

Or, you can look in the Yellow Pages under listings for specific services, such as Meals on Wheels, Visiting Nurses Associations, Homemaker-Home Health Aide Services, etc. The National Home-Caring Council provides a state-by-state list of its accredited home-maker/home health aide services. The National League of Nursing also has a list of its own accredited agencies. (You will find addresses for both at the end of this chapter.) Remember that initiating contact with any of the above-mentioned organizations or their counterparts can help bring you into the full network of home care services. So don't hesitate to make the initial contact and, if that doesn't bring results, keep trying.

Shopping for Quality Home Care

Navigating the maze of public and private agencies and services may seem an immense and bewildering task. But remember, despite shortages of these services, you are the customer in a highly competitive service industry. Shopping for a good agency is not unlike shopping in a supermarket. To your own experience as a consumer, add the following guidelines:

Choose an agency that evaluates your home situation before recommending a plan and assigning personnel. The agency should arrange to visit you to assess the situation, after a preliminary phone conversation. A good agency does not oversell its services. If you feel you are being given a hard sell on the phone for more service than you really need, be firm in ending the discussion. (You can always say you will get back to the agency after thinking it over.)

One way you can help the agency do a better job of evaluating your needs or those of your older relative is to fill out the Health Status and Health Services checklists in Appendix A before calling. Or, you may prefer to have someone who knows you well join with you in filling them out. This step will give you a solid basis for your contacts with agencies and make these contacts more effective.

Be sure you have a clear understanding of exactly what services are being offered. The homemaker/home health aide is not a maid. Ask for a specific list of the tasks that will be performed. If something important to you is omitted, ask about it. Even if the agency cannot fill that particular need, they may recommend someone who can.

As we mentioned earlier, some agencies supervise and train the worker placed in your home and take responsibility for the worker's performance. (For example, if a worker fails to show up one day, the agency will replace him/her with another person.) Some people would rather rely on an agency supervisor to apply professional standards and to deal fairly with any complaints that may arise. Other people prefer to deal directly with the employee in their own homes. If you have strong preferences in either direction, be sure to discuss with the agency *who* is responsible for training and monitoring the homemaker/home health aide, so you end up with the kind of supervision *you* want.

Before you hire an aide, make certain that you have at least two references from prior employers. As with anyone you bring in to work in your home, you will want to have assurances of the person's character and integrity. Although the agency may have conducted its own reference check, it is important to double check in this important area.

Whether the agency is run for profit or not is not necessarily related to the quality of its work. Accreditation is the best assurance of quality for a home-care agency. Don't confuse accreditation with licensing or certification. Being licensed and/or certified by the state may be necessary for the agency to operate but does not reliably assure quality.

The best sign that you are dealing with a competent and honest agency is accreditation by either the National HomeCaring Council or the National League of Nursing. Ask the person whom you first contact at the agency if they are accredited by either of these two organizations. If you have doubts about an agency you are dealing with, your local Better Business Bureau may also be of help.

One of your most valuable aids will be an excellent booklet—short and packed with useful information—titled "All About Home Care: A Consumer's Guide." This excellent, up-to-date booklet is produced by the National HomeCaring Council, Inc., a nonprofit organization devoted to developing services, monitoring standards, and educating consumers. The booklet is published cooperatively with the Council of Better Business Bureaus and is available at cost. (See address at the end of this chapter.)

Besides providing basic facts and elaborating on important details about home care, the Council's booklet includes a checklist of questions to ask when contacting and dealing with home-care agencies. For each question or situation, appropriate follow-up action is suggested, to confirm that the agency is as represented and will fulfill its obligations to you. The booklet also offers practical advice on negotiating financial arrangements, dealing with home-care personnel, and avoiding many common problems before they have a chance to develop. A down-to-earth discussion of how to handle problems that do sometimes arise in home care effectively is most helpful.

How Can You Pay For Home Care?

There are a number of ways to pay for different kinds of home care and some people are able to combine more than one method. Costs for different services range from the inexpensive to very costly, but are almost always less than hospital or nursing home costs. The following forms of payment are most likely to apply if you or a family member are over 65:

Medicare can be used by everyone over 65 and by certain disabled persons *under* 65. It pays for part-time skilled nursing, physical therapy, and speech therapy. If any one of these three services is used, Medicare sometimes pays for limited amounts of needed part-time homemaker/home health aide services, medical social services, occupational therapy and some medical supplies and equipment. All of these services must be ordered by a physician and all services must be provided by a certified home health agency. New rules affecting the scope of Medicare coverage are currently being worked out. To get this and other information about Medicare, call your local social security office.

Medicaid is designed for low-income people of all ages. It is administered by each of the fifty states, so that rules for coverage vary somewhat from one to another. Medicaid covers a number of expenses not included under Medicare. Rules and benefits under Medicaid may also be changing in the near future. Your local social security office can give you further information, as can your city or county Department of Social Services.

Private health insurance through nonprofit companies such as Blue Cross/Blue Shield (and through some of the commercial insurers), covers certain home care services. Not all policies spell these provisions out. Contact the insurer to find out exactly what your policy includes in the way of health-related home care. You may be able to combine private insurance and Medicare or Medicaid to obtain the range of services you need.

Health Maintenance Organizations (HMOs) often include some types of home care in their health care packages. If you belong to a prepaid health plan, you should, again, inquire specifically as well as re-read your contract carefully.

Title XX (Twenty) of the Social Security Act as well as certain provisions of the Older Americans Act of 1965 may help support homemaker/home health aide services for some low-income older people. As before, your local social security office or State Office on Aging can supply fuller information.

Self payment—out-of-pocket expenses for some types of home care (home nursing, special equipment and transportation to health centers)—may be tax deductible, whether you are paying for yourself or someone else. (The other person need not be your dependent.) IRS publication 502, "Medical and Dental Expenses," explains further, or you can call your local Internal Revenue Service office—preferably not near the April 15th tax deadline.

Day Programs

There are some older people for whom in-home services are not the answer, but who need some outside assistance in maintaining daily independence. Senior centers or a day program may fill the bill for you. Or, you may want to use them in combination with a specific type of in-home service. Despite recent cutbacks in the number and size of day programs, an estimated 10,000 senior centers and 12,000 nutrition programs operate nationwide.

If you are over 55 years old, some type of day program for older people may be available for you at a local community center. Some programs focus on social, educational, and recreational activities. Others (often affiliated with a hospital) offer rehabilitative therapy and nursing consultation as well. Many serve a nutritious midday meal, and virtually all can help participants and their families reach other community-based services which can benefit them.

Day programs for people 55 and over operate on a nonprofit basis and cost $20-$26 per day, which typically includes one hot meal. However, you may not have to pay the full amount. Fees are paid on a sliding scale, according to income, or may be handled through Medicaid.

To find a senior citizen center or day hospital in your local community, the telephone directory may be your best bet. Look in the yellow pages under the heading, "Day Center for Older Persons." If this does not produce results, a call to any of the following probably will: your local State Office on Aging (see Appendix D), the American Red Cross, United Way, the Discharge Planning or Home Care Department of your local hospital, Jewish Family Services, Catholic Charities, or any social service agency or hot line.

Temporary Respite Care

Sometimes older people manage well as things are, but find that life is occasionally disrupted by an unexpected change or emergency. Temporary respite care can provide a solution. What are some of the circumstances in which you might want to use respite care? Here are a few examples:

• You live with or depend on family members who are leaving on a vacation or business trip for a little while.

- Someone you depend on for assistance becomes ill or must be hospitalized.

- You live alone and experience an emergency, such as a robbery, a fire, or a utility failure. You need a comfortable place to stay until things are repaired or returned to normal.

Respite care is a new innovation, designed to help people fill these periodic needs. According to Temp Care, a Bronx, New York, non-profit program, respite can take any of the following forms:

Respite in your own home. This involves sending someone to stay with an older person while family members are away on vacation or on business. This arrangement can help give the family periodic "time off" while making sure the older person's needs are taken care of.

Care in an outside, homelike place. If family members are away for a week or two, it may be more convenient and pleasant for an older person to spend the time somewhere other than home. Small, home-like respite facilities offer meals, activities and company. Outside programs can also fill in during a temporary housing emergency.

Medical respite. While most respite is not for people who require nursing or convalescent care, a few programs connected with medical facilities have opened up. These programs are for people with illnesses who are normally cared for at home by a relative or friend. Medical respite gives caregivers an opportunity for a rest and some time off every so often. It can help them to continue longer in their caregiving roles, so that the person who is ill can remain at home as long as possible.

Respite care is a new concept, and not all states and localities provide it. Estimates of cost are also incomplete at this point. In-home respite care given by homemakers or companions can cost about $6-$8 per hour, while a home health aide's fee ranges upwards of $8 hourly. Respite care outside the home may average around $60 per day, while medical respite involving skilled nurses may average about $80. However, respite is usually paid for out-of-pocket on a sliding scale pegged to your income, so these figures are not necessarily what *you* would be charged. To find out whether respite care is available in your locality and to get answers to other important questions, call your county or state Department of Social Services.

Home Sharing: A Different Strategy For Staying Put

A very different sort of strategy for staying put, despite mounting expenses or health limitations, is home sharing. Home sharing has been carried on informally for a long time by people of all ages. It is not at all unusual for relatives or friends to live together in order to reduce expenses, provide extra security, lighten housekeeping burdens and exchange support or care during difficult periods. We know that different generations sometimes share—for example, an adult child in his or her sixties and a parent in his or her eighties. You can also share a home with people other than your immediate family. It is an option offering many advantages, in addition to affordability.

What is Home Sharing?

Home sharing is an arrangement in which two or more unrelated people have their own private space while sharing other areas of a house or apartment in common.

Most of the time, home sharing involves a home provider and a home seeker, who agree on a mutual living arrangement. In many communities, non-profit match-up programs (as well as commercial housemate services) help compatible providers and seekers find each other and negotiate a home sharing agreement.

Another kind of shared housing is a group residence. This type of home is seldom owned by any one of its residents, and is usually sponsored by a nonprofit local community group. We will discuss this kind of sharing in Chapter Four.

Would Home Sharing Work For You?

The most important requirement for home sharing is that both parties really prefer living with another person.

You don't have to remodel your home to adapt it for sharing. Most of the time, no significant renovation is done. Once in awhile, a homeowner does make some changes, such as adding a bath or separate entry, to insure privacy. A one-family house or large apartment can easily be shared. If you or an older relative are the sole occupant of a good-sized, rent-controlled apartment, you may be a good home provider. If you have decided to give up your too-large, too-expensive home or apartment, you are in an excellent position to choose a housemate from among those providing space in many different kinds of homes.

Home sharing offers advantages to people in different life circumstances. Sharing does bring down living costs. A 1982 study in the Baltimore-Washington, D.C., area showed that the annual cash saving to homeowner and tenant averaged about $1800 apiece. Many sharing arrangements involve exchanges of services as well as a financial transaction. This is especially the case when one party is experiencing some health limitations. Home sharing might be good for you if you cannot manage entirely alone, but require only limited or occasional assistance on a daily basis.

When Sophie Monroe had surgery on her leg, she knew it would take a while to heal because she has osteoarthrosis. "When I left the hospital," she says, "they told me I could go to a convalescent home, but I was very reluctant to do so." Instead, she "staggered along" at home in a thick cast with the help of a friend who came over two hours a day, four days a week. A Meals-on-Wheels-type program brought meals in five days a week. On weekends, however, there were no meals. "If my friends weren't around, I was marooned," she says. "I'm not wealthy—I couldn't afford to hire help."

However, she does have an extra bedroom in her apartment. About that time, she saw a notice in her church bulletin pinned there by a woman willing to exchange services for room and board. Sophie called. "But it didn't work out." The woman had two small children—too many people for Ms. Monroe's two-bedroom apartment. Still, she didn't give up.

Her church referred her to Independent Living, Inc.'s Project Home Share. After she called, someone from the Project visited her for an informal interview. Not long after, they sent her three prospective roommates, all of whom were interested in sharing Sophie's home. Her choice was Fran Miller, a law student.

Project Home Share helped negotiate a contract between the two women. Fran does not pay rent; instead, she does two and a half hours of work each day for Sophie. "Fran drives, takes messages, does my shopping, mails my Christmas presents, and does things around the house that I can't do," says Sophie, who will have to be on crutches for nine or ten months after her cast is off.

"'With Fran,'" she says, "I can keep my life much closer to normal—I can ignore my problems most of the time." Fran Miller is 30 years old. Sophie is 70. "I enjoy having her here," says Sophie, "It's worked out pretty well."

Many people become interested in this option during a time of change and transition: recent loss of a spouse, of work, income, health or home. The Baltimore sharers who were studied reported an increased sense of security and well being as a result of having another person in the house. Even if you have not had a recent significant loss or health problem, you may want to consider home sharing because of its potential for increasing security and well being and because it is economical.

Setting Up a Shared Housing Arrangement

How can you link up with compatible people who want to share? And how can you arrive at a realistic and fair agreement? You can, of course, meet a housemate through mutual acquaintances, through church or civic groups or through an advertisement. Most people who share hesitate to take the risks involved in these methods.

Another, safer and more thorough way to find a compatible housemate is through a nonprofit match-up program specializing in the needs of older adults. (You can also use a commercial housemate referral service, but these provide a less individual approach.) A state-by-state listing of match-up programs and housemate referral services is available from the Shared Housing Resources Center. (See the end of this chapter for their address.)

Match-up programs offer a range of services. You don't have to use all of them, but most people do prefer to. Most programs begin with a visit to the home offered for sharing. Both the home provider and the home seeker are interviewed, confidentially, about their housing and health needs. The interview also provides an opportunity to discuss expectations and concerns about home sharing. This process also helps you balance the pros and cons of sharing, as you set about meeting potential housemates and making your decision. Project SHARE, a Nassau County, New York, program, has matched approximately 600 persons in this way.

Assistance is provided by some programs in negotiating an oral or written agreement with your housemate. Follow-up services may also be available to help you solve any differences that may arise or to nip problems in the bud.

How Home Sharing Affects Living Expenses

Since economy is a major motive in home sharing, here are some details that will help you calculate the effects of sharing on your personal budget.

Rent and utilities are typically divided among housemates on an equitable basis. In most cases, *food costs* are also shared, often resulting in savings to each individual.

It is important to know, too, about other less obvious savings and costs:

Your *property taxes*, under some conditions, may be affected by house sharing, if you are the home provider. In many states, taxes are based on the assessed value of both house and land and have nothing to do with the number of people occupying the house. However, if you change the physical structure of the house (remodel or subdivide it)—you may find that the assessed value has changed, and, with it, your tax.

Do you receive *"circuit-breaker" tax credits?* Those are tax breaks for people whose property taxes or rents are high in relation to their income. Your credit is determined by household gross income, which would be increased by adding more people to your household. If the new household members live in separate apartments, your credit will not be affected.

Social Security payments are not affected by home sharing, but *Supplemental Security Income (SSI)* can be reduced by payments received as rent. These benefits can be reduced even if your tenant performs services (such as helping with chores) instead of paying rent. Likewise, if you receive SSI and you sell or rent your home to move in with someone else, your benefits could be reduced because of the money you received from the sale or rent of your previous home. Legislation is currently under consideration that could relax some of these regulations. Check with your local social security office for the most current information.

If you receive *food stamps*, your allocation could be changed because of home sharing. The government considers any household in which food is purchased and prepared together as a single household and will allot only one set of food stamps per household. However, if you only share kitchen facilities—not food—your food stamp allocations will not be affected. These rules too are being relaxed; check with the Department of Social Services in your city or county.

Homeowners' insurance is not affected by home sharing, but it does not cover the personal property of the person entering the household, who will need to have renter's insurance.

Don't forget to calculate all of the above costs that apply to you and balance them against the financial gains of sharing.

Zoning Laws

While home sharing is on the increase, it was not taken into account when most local zoning ordinances were written. Zoning ordinances in some single-family neighborhoods actually prohibit sharing between unrelated persons or the payment of rent by one to another.

To see if this problem applies in your community, go to your nearest library and look at the "Definition" section in your local zoning ordinance. Note the precise definition of a "family," a "roomer" or a "boarder." If you change the physical structure of your house or land, you may need to get the approval of your zoning board. If you don't make structural changes and the only problem is in the "Definition" section, you can request a legal variance. Be sure to do this *before* you start home sharing, if your community is one that has a restrictive definition.

In many single-home communities, a move is now under way to either change zoning laws or to establish fair standards for making exceptions. If you want to share your home with another older person, chances are very good that you can obtain a variance or permit from your town council or housing office.

In sum, home sharing may enable you or an older relative to remain within home and community at a time when continued independence may be uncertain. Under most circumstances, it can reduce living expenses while fulfilling a number of physical, social and emotional needs. But, if you have to give up too much, the costs may outweigh the advantages.

It is important to compare what you gain to what you lose. Home sharing is a special kind of interdependence in which two individuals help each other to live independently as long as possible. If it is to work, both parties must clearly want the arrangement. At the same time sharing is *not* a lifetime contract; should you decide to try something else, you are always free to do so. Increasing numbers of older Americans from all walks of life are deciding that it is a venture worth trying.

Key Resources

Home Equity Conversion Plans

National Center for Home Equity Conversion will furnish a brochure explaining home equity conversion, copies of their newsletter and other information. Write:

> Ken Scholen
> National Center for Home Equity Conversion
> (NCHEC)
> 110 East Main Street
> Room 1010
> Madison, WI 53703

Information is also available from American Association of Retired Persons. Write:

> Leo Baldwin
> Consumer Housing Information Service
> American Association of Retired Persons (AARP)
> 1909 K Street, NW
> Washington, DC 20049

The American Bar Association will send a free copy of its pamphlet entitled 'Home Equity Conversion? Consumer Facts.' They are also developing model legal documents. Write:

American Bar Association
Commission on Legal Problems of the Elderly
1800 M Street, NW
Washington, DC 20036

Home Care Services

The National HomeCaring Council and the Better Business
Bureau copublish an excellent booklet entitled, "All About
Home-Care: A Consumer's Guide," available for cost at $2.00.
Write:

National HomeCaring Council, Inc.
235 Park Avenue South
New York, NY 10003
(212) 674-4990

Information is also available from:

National League for Nursing
10 Columbus Circle
New York, NY 10019
(212) 582-1022

National Association for Home Care
519 C Street, NE
Washington, DC 20002

American Red Cross
Main Office
2025 E Street, NW
Washington, DC 20006
(202) 737-8300

The previous two listings can provide information about education
and training for homemaker/home health aide positions.

Information about home-care services affiliated with hospitals is
available from:

Joint Commission on Accreditation of Hospitals (JCAH)
875 North Michigan Avenue
Chicago, IL 60611

Home-Sharing and Match-up Services or Programs

Shared Housing Resource Center acts as a national information clearinghouse and publishes a national directory of match-up programs and housemate referral services. Ask for their free information packet.
A self-help guide, "Is Home Sharing for You?" is also available for $3. Write:

Shared Housing Resource Center
6344 Greene Street
Philadelphia, PA 19144
(215) 848-1220

Action for Boston Community Development has published two excellent booklets (in large print) on shared living: an individual planning guide and a community planning guide for groups that want to organize a small shared living situation. Write:

Action for Boston Community Development
178 Tremont Street
Boston, MA 02111
(617) 357-6000

References

Action for Boston Community Development, *Shared Living: A Community Planning Guide*. Boston, 1982.

_____, *Shared Living: An Individual Planning Guide*. Boston, 1982.

American Association of Retired Persons, 1983 Federal and State Legislative Policy and 1983-1984 State Legislative Committee Policy Guidelines, Washington, D.C., 1984. See especially pp. 83 and 108.

Cabin, Bill, Statistical Researcher, National Association of Home Care, personal communication, August 1985.

Chi, Judy, "Home Health Care: No Longer a Cottage Industry," *Drug Topics*, December 12, 1983:68-69.

Cohen, Elias, "Caveats for Home Equity Conversion," *The Coordinator*, July 1984:32-33.

Day-Lower, Dennis, D. Bryant, et al., "Shared Housing," in *Housing Options for Older Americans*. Washington, D.C.: American Association of Retired Persons, 1984.

Demkovich, Linda, "In Treating the Problems of the Elderly, There May Be No Place Like Home," *National Journal*, December 22, 1979:2154-58.

Dobkin, Leah, "Home Matching Programs," in *Housing Options for Older Americans*. Washington, D.C.; American Association of Retired Persons, 1984.

_____, "Shared Housing Match-Up Programs: Transforming Housing Units Into Homes." Philadelphia; Shared Housing Resource Center, 1982.

Drake, Jerry, Tax Economist, Oregon State Legislative Research Library, Legislative Revenue Office, personal communication, August 1985.

Hare, Patrick, and M. Haske, "Innovative Living Arrangements: A Source of Long-Term Care," *Aging*, December/January 1983-1984:3-8.

Hareven, Tamara, "The Family as Process: The Historical Study of the Family Cycle," *Journal of Social History*, Spring 1974:322-329.

"The Home Health Care Boom," *New York Times*, June 30, 1983.

"Home Health Care: New Forces Propel Home Health-Care Market," *Drug Topics*, July 4, 1983:77-78.

Hurley, Gertie, "Careers in Home Health Care," *Washington Post*, March 31, 1982.

Inz, Jessie, Director, Project Share, Family Service Association of Nassau County, N.Y., personal communication, August 1985.

Kimmel, Howard, and P. Pollak, (eds.), *Shared Housing: A Community Based Option. A Compendium of Speeches from Workshops on Planning and Developing Home Sharing Programs.* Ithaca, N. Y.: Cornell Cooperative Extension, New York State Division of Housing and Community Renewal, January 1984.

Kleyman, Paul, "Home Equity: A Resource for Home Care and Independence for the Elderly," *The Coordinator*, July 1984:28-29.

Levenson, Marjorie, "Intergenerational Housemate Matching: An Analysis of the Operations Match Program," paper presented at the 35th Annual Meeting of the Gerontological Society, Boston, November 1982.

Malakoff, Laura, and P. Pollak, "Home Sharing: One Option for Reducing the Housing Costs of Older Homeowners," *Consumer Closeups*. Ithaca, N.Y.: Cornell Cooperative Extension, 1982-83.

McConnell, Stephen, and C. Usher, *Intergenerational House Sharing*. Los Angeles: Andrus Gerontology Center, University of Southern California, 1980.

_____, The Conservation Foundation, personal communication, August 1985.

Meltzer, Judith, *Respite Care: An Emerging Family Support Service*. Washington, D.C.: The Center for the Study of Social Policy, 1982.

Michaelson, K., Assistant Director, National Institute of Senior Centers, National Council on Aging, personal communication, August 1985.

Myers, Phyllis, *Aging in Place: Strategies to Help the Elderly Stay in Revitalizing Neighborhoods*. Washington, D.C.: The Conservation Foundation, 1982.

National HomeCaring Council, *All About Home Care: A Consumer's Guide*. New York, 1982.

Osborn, Kevin, Information Specialist, States Information Center, Council of State Governments, personal communication, August 1985.

Priestman, Shawna, "Respite Care Meets a Desperate Need for Many Families," *Aging*, March/April 1983:31.

Pritchard, David, "The Art of Matchmaking," *Gerontologist*, 23:174-79, 1983.

Ranson, Betty, Director, National Institute of Senior Centers, National Council on Aging, personal communication, August. 1985.

"Respite: A Visiting Resident Program," Respite Care Program, Metropolitan Jewish Geriatric Center, Brooklyn, N. Y. brochure, n.d.

Scholen, Ken, "Home Equity Conversion," in *Housing Options for Older Americans*. Washington, D.C.: American Association of Retired Persons, 1984.

Schreter, Carol, "House Sharing by Non-Frail Older Persons," in *Housing Options for the Community Resident Elderly: Policy Report of the Housing Choices of Older Americans Study*. Bryn Mawr, Pa.: Bryn Mawr College, 1982.

————, "Room for Rent: Home Sharing With Nonrelated Older Americans," Ph.D. dissertation, Bryn Mawr College, Bryn Mawr, Pa., 1983.

————, "Residents of Shared Housing," *Social Thought*, Winter 1984:30-38.

Schwartz, Richard, "Day Care Center Brings New Perspective to Mt. Vernon Elderly," *Aging*, March/April 1983.

Shared Housing Quarterly, Vol. 1, No. 1, July 1982.

Shared Housing Quarterly, Vol. 2, No. 1, March 1984.

Shared Housing Resource Center, *National Directory of Shared Housing Programs for Older People*. Philadelphia, 1983.

"Temp Care," Temp Care, Aging in America, Bronx, N. Y., brochure, n.d.

U.S. Bureau of the Census, "Current Population Reports," Series P-20, No. 398, U.S. Government Printing Office, Washington, D.C., 1984.

U.S. Bureau of the Census, "Current Population Reports," Series P-23, No. 128, U.S. Government Printing Office, Washington, D.C., 1983.

U.S. Department of Energy, Residential Energy Consumption Survey.

Wells, Charles, Deputy Commissioner, U.S. Administration on Aging, personal communication, August 1985.

White House Conference on Aging, Report of the Mini-Conference on Housing for the Elderly, Washington, D.C., 1981.

White House Conference on Aging, Summary Reports of the Committee Chairmen, Washington, D.C., December 3, 1981.

Wilner, Mary Ann, and J. Witkin, "Shared Living for Elders: A Viable Alternative," *Challenge!*, U.S. Department of Housing and Urban Development, Washington, D.C., September 1980.

Woodward, Anne, "Housing the Elderly," *Society*, Vol. 19, January/February 1982:52-57.

Chapter 3

Living Near, Not With The Children

Accessory Apartments And Echo Housing

Independence and self-sufficiency are two characteristics of living that most older people value intensely. But what if you want to live independently and yet still have the support and companionship of close relatives nearby? There are ways to live near your children—or other relatives—without actually moving in with them. We will be looking in this chapter at two such options: first, at a way of subdividing living space into two private apartments and then at an innovative living arrangement known as "echo housing," temporary living units for older persons that can be installed on the property of a single family home. Each contains high potential for substantially improving the life situation of participants and each can be accomplished without extensive bureaucratic involvement or public expense.

Accessory Apartments: A Modern Version Of An Old Idea

An accessory apartment is created when the owner of a single-family home converts it by installing a complete new living unit. Accessory apartments do not involve any shared space except, possibly, an outer entry hall or outdoor space. Accessory apartments can be used as rental units but are often created specifically to accommodate the needs of older people.

Accessory apartments are new in name only. We have all heard of people who remodel their homes to produce what is popularly called the "in-law suite," usually used for the owner's parents. Sometimes older homeowners convert unused space in their houses to accomodate young relatives or renters. This use of accessory apartments has been advocated as a way to help older people on fixed incomes tap into their greatest unused resource, their homes. Although not an innovation itself, it has recently received much media attention because of its innovative potential in resolving housing shortages and other problems affecting all age groups.

There are no available statistics to tell us how many homes across the country have been converted in this way. "Guesstimates" range from one million upward. Patrick Hare, a Washington, D.C., housing and planning consultant who has written extensively about housing alternatives, estimates that roughly 1.5 million exist. While these statistics are hardly adequate, they are the best clues we have to the prevalence of accessory apartments in the United States.

Costs of Accessory Housing

Patrick Hare states that the typical conversion cost for the type of home likely to be converted is about $10,000. Obviously, the size, shape and layout of the original home will determine whether or not it makes financial sense to install an apartment. Based on a $10,000 estimate, the monthly home improvement loan payment (principal plus interest plus insurance and taxes) would rarely exceed $200—well below the rental income from most apartments of comparable size.

Adult children who create an accessory apartment for a parent could allow the parent to live there free of charge, but a great many older people would also be willing and able to cover this modest monthly expenditure. Older homeowners who create an apartment could be enlarging their own incomes while offering a student, a new jobholder, or newly married children a modestly priced place to live. In some cases, the tenant could be offered a break in rent in exchange for performing maintenance or other chores.

Benefits to Residents

Besides the economic advantages just mentioned, accessory apartments offer security and safety, by virtue of having other people close by. If you are concerned about having help in an emergency or about cutting down on travel time between family members while still preserving privacy for both, you may want to seriously consider this living arrangement.

If you spend part of the year in a warm climate or travel fairly extensively, knowing that you have left someone behind in your house can be very reassuring. Other advantages include potential companionship, access to mutual support, and above all, preservation of privacy and independence. Many people who share homes or create apartments arrange with the occupant for household and transportation services in lieu of part or all of the rent. In many cases, these services can make it possible for an older person to continue managing on his or her own for many years.

Furthermore, if you are the one providing the accessory apartment, a disruptive move can be averted altogether. And, even if you are moving into an accessory apartment in someone else's house, you may be able to stay within the same neighborhood, minimizing separation and loss caused by relocating to a new community. Moving into an accessory apartment belonging to an adult child in another city or state is, of course, a much more serious disruption, to be weighed carefully against the potential advantages of being near close kin.

Neighborhood and Community Impact

One of the more impressive benefits of accessory apartments is the fact that they represent an efficient and productive use of existing housing. Virtually all accessory housing we know of has sprung up in the suburbs. In an era of rental shortages and uncertain housing starts, this is a strong selling point. Another strong point is that accessory apartments involve little or no exterior change to the house, thus preserving the visual appearance of the neighborhood.

According to the Bureau of the Census, many older Americans are "overhoused" in terms of space, while others have difficulty finding any suitable housing at all. As of 1984, over 13 million owner-occupied houses were inhabited by people over the age of 65. In most of these cases, one or two people are living in homes designed to accommodate a more sizeable family group. Accessory apartments could result in worthwhile use of this housing stock.

Another significant advantage to both users and communities is that accessory apartments need virtually no public subsidy. You need not become involved with any social service bureaucracy or commercial agent to provide yourself or a relative with this type of living arrangement. Accessory apartments represent a purely private solution.

Zoning Laws and Other Problems

Accessory apartments can entail some pitfalls. Zoning laws in most communities traditionally prohibit conversion of single-family housing to multiple dwellings, making most of the estimated 1.5 million accessory apartments in the U.S. technically illegal. But in many communities, these regulations are undergoing changes toward greater flexibility. Phyllis Myers of the Conservation Foundation, who has also written about housing alternatives, notes that accessory apartments are often accepted within most communities as long as members of the added household are related to the owner. Acceptance is even more easily won if either the homeowners or the new apartment tenants are parents of the home's other occupants.

Nevertheless, opposition to accessory apartments cannot be ignored. Most opposition centers around fears that the apartments could lead to a transient neighborhood population, to poor maintenance and to an eventual drop in property values. These fears are most realistic in cases of absentee ownership, but are much less well founded when one of the units is owner-occupied.

Another objection to accessory apartments is that the added population creates a drain on community services (schools, police, sanitation) without contributing to the tax base that supports those services—in other words, tenants of accessory apartments may get a "free ride" at the expense of neighborhood homeowners. This may be a valid objection in some cases, but on the whole, most communities were planned and constructed when expected population density was at a peak. Suburban population has now declined and many businesses and schools, for example, would gladly welcome a new influx of residents.

Taking Down the Barriers

In order to bring accessory apartments into the mainstream of American housing, we need to find fair and practical solutions to the problems discussed above. Most writers on the subject think a search for solutions is worthwhile because the concept of accessory apartments for older people is, basically, such a sensible one.

A recent California state law now requires all communities to zone for accessory apartments. Some other communities have moved toward legalizing accessory apartments by rewriting existing regulations or creating criteria for special permits. Some communities that have made such changes are: Babylon, Long Island; Westport, Connecticut; Boulder, Colorado; and Portland, Oregon. In other communities, such as Hartford, Connecticut, the issue of accessory apartments was raised but went down to defeat. But the general trend seems to be that more and more local communities are falling in line behind this innovation.

Legal changes sometimes come about when a community realizes that an impressive percentage of the single family homes in it have already been converted. In Babylon, Long Island, so many illegal accessory apartments were springing up that the town bowed to reality and accepted those that met specific criteria. The town of Westport, Connecticut legalized accessory apartments only in cases where both owners and tenants were over 62 years of age—a solution which does not benefit most adult children who share this form of housing with aged parents. (The town planner for Westport has stated that only about a third of the estimated 800 accessory apartments in town are legal.)

In general, zoning changes have included safeguards against inequities and possible abuse. Patrick Hare suggests these guidelines for zoning changes:

- Permit conversions only by owner-occupants.

- Prohibit or minimize exterior changes (such as additional front entrances) that change the neighborhood's visual character.

- Reach out to local realtors, civic associations and other groups who can benefit from accessory apartments, such as older adults, single parents, and the handicapped.

- Small communities, instead of rewriting existing laws, can grant variances on a case-by-case basis.

A few unsolved problems still remain. For example, what will happen to the accessory apartment when the elderly occupant leaves or dies? Or when the property is sold? And what about increased tax liabilities? Isolated reports suggest that such homes have been seen as desirable and have sold ahead of the general market, but reliable and complete evidence is not yet in. The town of Babylon, L.I. found that the average tax increase resulting from conversions was $115, a figure which does not seem prohibitive. Are accessory apartments worth the complications? Several housing consultants feel they are and suggest that the best people to carry on the move toward complete acceptance are older homeowners themselves. Older homeowners are not likely to be accused of wanting to run down neighborhoods in which they have spent a large part of their lives. They not only would be acting out of enlightened self-interest but would be freeing untapped resources to serve increasing needs for living space by more and more Americans.

If you are interested in creating an accessory unit in your home, or in contacting someone else who has, write to one of the groups listed at the chapter's end.

Echo Housing — Alias "Granny Flats"

Echo housing is an innovation that carries accessory housing several steps further. The term "echo house" describes a small, temporary living unit for older persons, installed on the property of a single-family home. Echo housing has been advocated as a good way for adult children to take care of older parents who need some degree of support and aid in a way that respects the independence of both households. It has also been suggested that older homeowners could move into smaller "echo" units installed on their property, renting out the original houses to younger relatives or friends as a way of boosting income. The idea originated in Australia, where single-family homes and zoning laws similar to our own prevail. In Australia, these small, moveable cottages were popularly nicknamed "granny flats," and were rented to individuals by the government. Estimates say that about 500 are currently in use.

The concept traveled to this country by way of England, where it has also been tried experimentally. One of the first steps in Americanizing "granny" flats was to change their name. Leo Baldwin, housing consultant to the American Association of Retired Persons (AARP), points out that the term "granny flat" is inappropriate for men who might occupy this form of housing and, in fact, for some women as well. He suggests the term "echo housing" to replace it, though both terms continue to be used in the media.

Granny flats, elder cottages, and echo housing are all one and the same—to avoid confusion, we will use the term "echo housing." It is important, though, to understand the difference between echo housing and accessory apartments. While neither involve any shared space, the accessory apartment is a second unit or subdivision within the framework of an existing single house, seldom involving changes to the exterior. Echo housing, by whatever name, consists of a second unit separate from the existing house, standing on the same lot or acreage.

Not surprisingly, echo housing got its start here in rural and semi-rural areas, to which it is probably best suited. It was first introduced into Lancaster County, Pennsylvania, home of the Amish, who are noted for devotion to their elders. Peter Dys, an official in the Lancaster County Office of Aging, attempted unsuccessfully to find federal funding for a first project. A manufacturer in the local area began to produce modular units to be sold as "echo housing" but instead found a market for them among younger, first-time home buyers, who planned to place them in more densely settled areas.

While only a small number of echo housing units have actually-been placed in operation, the idea keeps resurfacing in the media and has drawn expressions of support from a number of organizations serving older people.

What Does Echo Housing Look Like?

Edward Guion, who has attempted to develop and market these cottages in Lancaster County, Pennsylvania, designed a prefabricated unit made of wood. The units conform to standard building codes. Guion recommends installing them on specially treated wood pilings (which resemble a traditional foundation) for easy removal. A one bedroom model contains 528 square feet. A 720 square foot, two-bedroom model as well as a 480 square foot efficiency model have also been designed. Additional rooms can be added on at any time. Each cottage has a living room, bedroom, bath, kitchen, pantry and utility area with washer and dryer. Special features include doors wide enough to accommodate a wheelchair, bathroom grab bars, low wall switches and electrical outlets placed at convenient height for wheelchair users. Exteriors may be of aluminum or vinyl siding, of stained wood or of white stucco board, to blend in with other homes in the neighborhood.

Costs: Now and Later

As of 1985, the price of these units were $11,980 for the efficiency, $19,600 for the one-bedroom and $23,575 for the two-bedroom models. At least another $2,500 is required for sitework and freight. The total cost compares well with the $48,000 construction cost for a unit of federally subsidized elderly housing. Heating costs in Pennsylvania, a cold state, are estimated at $365 yearly.

Estimated costs do not include landscaping, linkage to certain utilities such as wells or sewers, taxes, insurance and later removal costs. The small number of existing units have not been in use long enough to enable us to cite long-term estimates involving maintenance and repair. It should be noted that although tax deductions on home mortgages and home improvements can be taken, there are no specific deductions for remodeling to modernize or maintain a full-time echo unit.

When Is Echo Housing Appropriate?

What might be the chief advantages of echo housing? There are several to think about, especially if you want to live near, not with your relatives or friends. Echo housing is not suited to high-density urban or suburban areas. It is best adapted to rural areas, small towns or suburbs with extra-large lots. This is important because very little has been done to develop reasonably priced housing for older rural residents.

The prime benefit of echo housing is that, in the words of one developer, it provides "proximity with privacy." It enables older and younger generations to exchange companionship and assistance without sacrificing the independence of either. Echo housing can offer you the best features of extended family living without some of its drawbacks—such as loss of privacy and freedom in daily life.

Echo housing may avert a move to a new community if you or an aging parent have had to give up the family home. It can also help avoid or postpone entry into a nursing facility, if you or your parent has reached the point where chronic health problems diminish ability to carry on activities of daily living unaided. In return for the safety and security of having people close by, an older person may be able to give something in return. Child care, house sitting, and good companionship are but a few of the things older people can provide relatives their own age or of a younger generation, when they live this near. If occupants of the main house are away during the day or on vacation, they may find it reassuring to know that someone is keeping an eye on the house, tending to plants or to pets.

In some cases, older homeowners might decide to move from the "main house" to a smaller echo unit on their own property, renting out the larger home. This would minimize the disruption of moving, satisfy a need for smaller quarters requiring less maintenance, and enhance income through rent received. If you have considered moving to some type of "senior housing" but don't want to be housed exclusively with people your own age, moving to an echo unit on your own or someone else's property might be the solution to this problem.

"Living by herself was taking a toll on Mom, physically and financially," says Marian Burdine. She and her widowed, 80-year-old mother, Fay Johnstone, formerly lived a half-hour apart in rural Frederick County, Maryland. Says Mrs. Johnstone, "I was trying to make ends meet on my husband's Social Security and the little bit that I got from the Veteran's. Of course, I did sewing and baby sitting, but with everything going up and two acres to take care of, it was just too much."

Fay Johnstone considered taking in a boarder, but decided it wouldn't work out. "You just don't have the freedom and privacy," she says firmly. "They've always been important to me."

Neither did Mrs. Johnstone want to move in with her daughter. "When there are two families in the same home, there's always that tension," she explains.

A neighbor told Marion Burdine that Frederick County allows temporary mobile homes or modular units to be erected on single family lots, to house older family members in need of attention and care. This sounded like the solution to both mother's and daughter's need for "proximity with privacy."

Fay now lives in a mobile home located in her daughter's backyard. How has the arrangement worked? "I'm very well satisfied," says Fay Johnstone. "We both have our privacy. We help each other out . . . at times. I still go back down to where I lived. I miss my friends . . . (but) I do some visiting about twice a week." Things are easier financially, too, now that she has sold her house. "I can go out and buy something now without wondering, can I afford this or should I do without?"

For her children, the greatest benefit is peace of mind. "All of us were so worried about Mom being by herself," says Mrs. Burdine. "I enjoy having her near, but the most important thing is knowing she doesn't have to struggle. She's freer to do things now she's never been able to do before."

Benefits to Neighborhood and Community

Advocates of echo housing point out three benefits to the general community. First, by increasing access to family support, it can reduce demands on some health and social services within the community. Secondly, by keeping the community age-integrated, demands for other services, such as schools and youth programs, may be stabilized. Third and last, echo housing can provide small, low-cost rental units to people of all ages at a time when the demand far exceeds the supply.

Problems and Cautions—Quality and Property Values

Although echo housing/elder cottages have created quite a stir in the media, with stories in *McCall's*, *The Wall Street Journal*, *The New York Times*, *The Washington Post*, *Aging* magazine, and others, it has not caught on with the buying public. Because echo housing sounds like a worthwhile idea, it is important to understand the major objections to it and try to determine how well founded they are. Beyond that, some creative thinking is called for in dealing with those obstacles that are grounded in reality.

Two major problems have been raised in connection with echo housing. The greatest concern is that it will contribute to general neighborhood decline. And some writers on the subject caution against potential abuse by developers and builders.

Those who predict neighborhood decline often point to the mobile homes that cluster on the lands adjoining many major highways. While these mobile home settlements are perfectly acceptable features of the American landscape to some people, others consider them eyesores and fear that echo housing could create a similar problem.

How would echo housing affect the market value and saleability of the original house and land? Fears that the owner would be stuck with a white elephant have not yet been put to the test. But, as we will see in the next section, a simple solution to this potential problem has been proposed.

There are other reasons for caution on the part of potential buyers of echo units. While the demonstration units built in Lancaster County, Pennsylvania conform to code and have worn well since 1981, competitors have entered the field offering even lower prices. Consumers may be taken in by advertising and promotional campaigns, only to find they have bought shoddy materials and poor quality construction.

These and other problems have reinforced zoning ordinances in most communities that positively prohibit echo housing in single-family areas. Although thousands of inquiries about echo housing have been received by the original developer and by the American Association for Retired Persons (AARP), which has taken an interest, only a handful of units have been sold. The problems discussed here as well as a number of others have been blamed for the failure of echo housing to gain wide acceptance, but prohibitive zoning is most often mentioned as the chief deterrent.

Some proponents of echo housing believe that in addition to working for zoning changes, people can request temporary variances in existing laws. If you need instructions, contact one of the key resources listed at the end of this chapter, or get in touch with your local Office of Aging (see Appendix D). Changes in zoning should contain clauses protecting against neighborhood decline and property devaluation. Suggested clauses include:

- permitting echo units only for elderly or handicapped relatives of property owners;

- removing the echo unit when the occupant leaves or dies;

- making permits conditional on population density and lot size, to avoid overcrowding;

- stipulating that the exterior of the echo unit match the exterior of the main house.

Advocates of echo housing hope that assurances such as these will win over opponents in communities where echo housing might be placed.

Prospects for Industry Self-Regulation

It has also been suggested that the prefab housing industry voluntarily impose standards on itself for the interior and exterior construction of echo units. Enforcement of these standards would be left to the industry. Since it is in the industry's own interests to develop new markets, the industry may begin to monitor standards more carefully. However, voluntary industrial regulation and enforcement have had only limited success in the past, so there are few reasons to believe that it would work any more effectively today. Unfortunately, there are no easy solutions to problems of quality control as they affect privately developed echo housing.

The future of echo housing in this country is still uncertain. The fact that it has found some acceptance in rural and semirural communities is important, because of the extreme scarcity of elder housing in rural (as compared to urban and suburban) communities. Localities presently experimenting with echo housing include Rockingham, North Carolina; Frederick County, Maryland; Lancaster County, Pennsylvania; and the states of Vermont, Wisconsin, Colorado and California. These communities and any others that join them will bear watching.

Under the worst of conditions, echo housing could contribute to neighborhood deterioration and to worsening environments for residents of all ages. Under the best of conditions, echo housing offers solutions to some of the human and financial problems involved in aging. Specifically, it can contribute to mutual aid and support within extended families and between generations, as well as promoting neighborhood solidarity. A great deal depends on the effectiveness of the safeguards that accompany early experiments, and possibilities for duplicating them in other communities across the country.

Key Resources

Patrick Hare is one of the very few people in the country with broad knowledge about accessory apartments and echo housing. Send stamped, self-addressed envelope for a list of available materials. Also available at cost ($5, including postage) is a discussion, in question and answer form, entitled "Installing an Accessory Apartment in the Surplus Space in Your Single Family Home." (There is a $2 surcharge on orders that are not prepaid.) Mr. Hare is also preparing a book on accessory apartments which will be published by McGraw-Hill sometime during 1985. Write:

Patrick H. Hare Planning and Design
1707 P Street NW
Washington, DC 20036
(202) 234-1219

Extensive information on this topic is also available from:

Leo Baldwin
Consumer Housing Information Service
American Association of Retired Persons (AARP)
1909 K Street, NW
Washington, DC 20049

The developer of the original echo house unit or "elder cottage," is:

Edward Guion
Coastal Colony Corporation
Lancaster, Pennsylvania
(717) 655-6761

References

Brooks, Andree, "Wide Appeal for Accessory Apartments," *New York Times*, January 3, 1982.

Gillies, Jim, Owner, Share-a-Home, Inc., Winter Park, Florida, personal communication, August 1985.

Carp, Frances, "The Concept and Role of Congregate Housing for Older People," paper presented at First National Conference on Congregate Housing for Older People, Washington, D.C., 1977.

Guion, Edward, "Elder Cottages: A New Feature on the Housing Horizon," *Aging*, December/January 1983-1984.

_____, Costal Colony Corporation, Lancaster, Pennsylvania, personal communication, August 1985.

Hare, Patrick, "Accessory Apartments," in *Housing Options for Older Americans*. Washington, D.C.; American Association of Retired Persons, 1984.

_____, "Carving Up the American Dream," American Planning Association, *Planning*, Vol. 47, No. 7, July 1981.

_____, "Rethinking Single-Family Zoning: Growing Old in American Neighborhoods," *Journal of Continuing Social Work Education*, Summer 1981:32-35.

_____, "The Nation's Largest Untapped Housing Resource," _Christian Science Monitor_, August 19, 1981.

_____, "The Empty Nest as a Golden Egg," _Perspectives on Aging_, March/April 1982:21-23.

_____, "Innovative Living Arrangements and the Role of Agencies Serving the Elderly," _Human Development News_, U.S. Department of Health and Human Services, Washington, D.C., January 1983.

_____, "Echo Housing," in _Housing Options for Older Americans_. Washington, D.C.: American Association of Retired Persons, 1984.

_____, "The Future of Granny Flats," unpublished paper, available from Hare Planning and Design, Washington, D.C., n.d.

Hare, Patrick, and E. Rozov, "Pursuing the Potential of Accessory Apartments," _Real Estate Today_, May 1982:45-46.

Hodges, Samuel and E. Goldman, _Allowing Accessory Apartments_. Washington, D.C.: U.S. Department of Housing and Urban Development, Office of Policy Development and Research, October 1983.

Myers, Phyllis, _Aging in Place: Strategies to Help the Elderly Stay in Revitalizing Neighborhoods_. Washington, D.C.: The Conservation Foundation, 1982.

Porter, Sylvia, "Accessory Apartment Legalization Urged," _Washington Post_, March 6, 1982.

Reiger, Arthur, and D. Engel, _Granny Flats: An Assessment of Economic and Land Use Issues_. Washington, D.C.: U.S. Department of Housing and Urban Development, Office of Policy Development and Research, January 1983.

Shaman, Diana, "Rentals in One-Family Homes Rising," _New York Times_, September 12, 1982.

Shepherd, Paul, "Granny Flats' May Be the Answer," _Human Development News_, U.S. Department of Health and Human Services, August/September 1982.

Woodward, Anne, "Housing the Elderly," _Society_, Vol. 19, January/February 1982:52–57.

Zeldis, Nancy, "The Hidden Rental Market," _Fairfax Journal_, May 22, 1981.

Chapter 4

Group Living

From Small Residences To Large Apartment Complexes

Group living arrangements in which some or all of the residents are older people come in as many shapes and forms as the consumers and communities they serve. Commonly called "senior housing," most do take the form of apartment-style living. No one knows precisely how many units are presently operating. There are at least hundreds of thousands, but various estimates disagree, probably because different experts define senior housing differently and are not counting the same things!

Experts do agree on the fact that group living opportunities for older people are very much in demand, and that the supply cannot begin to keep pace with the rapidly expanding over-65 population. In particular, low-cost, federally subsidized apartments are in very short supply—some urban projects report waiting lists that run as long as ten years.

Is group living the right alternative for your or members of your family? Group living can offer companionship, security and a modest amount of assistance with tasks like cooking and cleaning for older people who are beginning to need some help with such activities—in many cases at low to moderate cost.

As the demand for affordable senior housing continues to increase, pressures may be applied on a national scale to institute new building programs. Meanwhile, despite the discouraging shortage, you may want to look into the major types of low- and moderate-cost senior housing available in your community or in other locations that interest you. If this option appeals to you, being well informed and applying early gives you and your loved ones a better chance of obtaining what you want. Besides, as we will see, some new and innovative forms of group living don't involve such long waiting periods.

Types of Low- or Moderate-Cost Group Living

In order to cut the subject of group living down to manageable size, we will divide it three ways: group residences, senior apartments, and enriched or assisted senior housing. (Unfortunately, these terms are sometimes used overlappingly and, in different parts of the country, different terms may apply to the same thing.) Some more expensive options for group living—retirement communities and life-care plans—are discussed in Chapter 5.

The terms group home and group residence usually refer to a single unit in which a number of unrelated people live. Many are single-family homes that have been converted so as to provide private living space as well as common space for residents. Occasionally, group homes consist of several attached, townhouse-type units. The units may be jointly owned by residents like those in Share-a-Home (see box) or in a co-op. Or they may be leased by a sponsoring non-profit organization that rents to residents. In these small-group arrangements, outside health or social services can be provided to individuals who need them, but are not provided to the entire dwelling as a unit. This is important to remember because some of the larger apartment complexes include such services under the monthly fee. Some group residences are for older people only, while in others, generations are mixed.

Share-A-Home in Winter Park, Florida, is a collection of cooperatively owned small-group residences for people in relatively good health. The first home was established in 1969 for a group of twenty. A few years later, the group incorporated to help other homes develop and to assist newly formed households. Presently, Share-a-Home

consists of ten households in suburban and semi-rural locations with about 125 residents all told.

Each home is owned by the Share-a-Home Association and sub-leased to the residents. Household responsibilities and expenses are divided among members. The homes were all developed from existing buildings, including a convent, a college dorm, a ranch house and an estate. Residents have private or shared bedrooms.

Each household is autonomous and makes its own rules. Some have hired a manager and other staff to help with housekeeping, shopping and cooking, laundry, and chauffering of the family car. Average monthly costs, including rent, food, maintenance, staff salaries and household expenses ranged between $485-$800 per person, as of 1985.

Billie Sullivan, a resident for eleven years of Share-a-Home, is enthusiastic: "I love this place and wouldn't live anywhere else. We have a wonderful staff, excellent meals and intelligent people here."

First and foremost, small group homes have been shown to be economical for residents, reducing costs of housing and other living expenses as well. While it is necessary to be independent and fairly active to enter a group home, this cooperative style of living is nonetheless well suited to older (and younger) people with some health limitations.

Typically, residents participate together in daily chores, with or without outside assistance. The potential for companionship and some mutual aid and support is high. Together with the home's community sponsors, residents also participate in day-to-day management decisions.

If you or a family member are interested in low-cost living with a small group of compatible people and in participating with housemates in everyday routines, this type of arrangement may work well. Group residences generally don't have long waiting lists, and there is no need to become involved with large, bureaucratic agencies.

Subsidized senior apartments are probably the best-known form of low-cost group residence. Senior apartments may range from a single building, housing 50 or so tenants, to a large complex in which as many as 300 people live. Originally, this type of housing was sponsored almost exclusively by nonprofit organizations (such as B'nai B'rith or church groups or civic associations; see box) but the market is now attracting some commercial developers. Senior apartments differ in their styles of operation, in their staffing and services and in their methods of financing and management.

B'nai B'rith Senior Citizens Housing Network consists of seventeen apartment buildings in fourteen cities around the country, with three more under construction. Built with the aid of federal and state funds, the apartments are owned and operated by corporations set up by B'nai B'rith groups in the communities where the buildings are located.

Buildings range in size from 100 to 300 units. Altogether, 4,000 independent older adults in good health are housed in these low-cost apartments, which have moderate-to-long waiting lists. The Housing Network is open to all ethnic groups, so that each building reflects the diverse makeup of the community in which it is located. Rents are low to moderate, ranging from $250-$500 a month, depending on resident's income, but rentals do not exceed 30 percent of annual income—the "safe and reasonable" limit defined by the government.

All apartments are self-contained units with their own dining areas and kitchens. Each complex includes recreational space, such as dining rooms, game rooms, lounges, snack bars, well-equipped arts and crafts rooms, libraries, groceries, and barber/beauty shops. Most are situated within walking distance of shopping and health-care centers, or else they provide daily bus service to these places.

Each complex also includes special design features for the physically handicapped. Call buttons, emergency systems, and security systems are available for all apartments. Some buildings have organized activity programs, but opportunities for social exchange and companionship are present at all locations. Some programs reach out to older people in the general community by opening up certain activities and classes to neighborhood residents. Exercise programs, dance, arts and crafts, current events discussion groups, music, bridge, cooking and moviegoing all help to build bridges.

Enriched housing, sheltered housing, and assisted housing (the term used will depend on what part of the country you live in) includes a concentrated mix of health and social services as part of the total housing package. If you or a family member have been experiencing health or energy limitations that make it necessary to cut back on important activities, this type of living arrangement may be highly workable. Most important, independence can be maintained as long as possible, either postponing or eliminating the need for nursing home care.

Sponsorship and Costs

How does a senior housing program get its start? Many are sponsored by private nonprofit agencies: Area Agencies on Aging, church groups, fraternal orders, neighborhood and civic groups, and local housing authorities or planning departments. The U.S. Department of Housing and Urban Development (HUD) also provides financing for such projects.

Some sponsors or developers design and build brand-new accommodations. Others buy or lease existing buildings, which are used as-is or modified to fit the needs of potential residents. Former schools, hotels, motels, and empty church-owned buildings have been converted into senior housing, as have commercial buildings and lofts. Some housing for low-income older people is partially subsidized by HUD under its Section 8 program. However, recent government policy has encouraged cooperation between the public and private sector with an increasing emphasis on private contributions.

Rentals for HUD-subsidized housing are calculated according to complex formulas. They are based primarily on annually updated "fair market rents" for each community and each type of dwelling unit. Nationwide, the lowest reported subsidized rent for 1985 is $156 for an efficiency apartment in Little River County, Arkansas, or Grant Parish, Louisiana. The highest is $960 for a four-bedroom apartment in Anchorage, Alaska. To find out about obtaining such housing and about the rental ranges that apply in your own community, call your local department of housing.

The smaller types of group residence can be organized with less red tape. In a few cases, interested individuals (with some legal assistance) have joined together or allied themselves with a local community sponsor to set up a group residence. Or, a community organization may reach out to interested older people, assist them in locating a suitable building, and advise with household organization and management. The assisting agency may purchase or lease the building itself or may advise the group concerning a joint purchase.

A few years ago, the Back Bay Aging Concerns Committee (BBACC), a small Boston grassroots group, obtained federal start-up money from its local Area Agency on Aging to establish cooperative housing. With additional grants and donations, it bought a small elevator building, which eventually came to house 14 residents.

Although the majority of residents are over 65, this housing cooperative includes people of all ages. Householders cooperate in selecting new entrants and in making other decisions. Everyone is expected to share at least one household task that is within his/her abilities.

One writer describes further how the program works: "Frailties and illness are dealt with much as they would be in a family or among good friends. As the ill or handicapped become frailer, they and other residents together decide their mutual threshold of endurance in terms of the individual's continued residence."

Attendance is required at one group dinner per week and at a weekly house meeting, where all decisions are made. A permanent house administration committee reports to the board of directors. Theoretically, this committee could be composed entirely of residents but in actuality includes some "outsiders" who volunteer professional help.

In 1983, BBACC opened a second small group residence, similar to the first except that residents participate less directly in management. A third residence will open in 1986. Rents range from $156 to $325 per month, including utilities.

Physical Design Features

The appearances, floor plans, age and condition of group housing vary greatly. The proportion of private to common space varies, as does the provision of special design considerations for people who are disabled. Most buildings are located near public transportation and commercial centers and most, at the time they were built, were located in relatively crime-free areas.

Most people tend to want their own private kitchen and bathroom. But to the extent that this "wet space" can be shared, construction costs and, ultimately, rent will be considerably lower. A greater proportion of shared space may really be an advantage when you consider how reassuring the nearby presence of other people can be when you are alone or perhaps recuperating from an illness.

The New York State Division of Housing and Community Renewal has come up with a design for a senior housing unit that combines a concern for privacy with efficient and economical use of shared space. Planned for four people, it is large enough to have conversation, eating and study areas. The unit contains four bedrooms, two baths (each used by two persons) and shared laundry, kitchen, central dining, living room, TV, lounge and storage areas. The kitchen is large enough to contain two work areas and two refrigerators.

Remember, *no* senior housing should be without safety features, such as grab bars, handrails and ramps, smoke detectors, and adequate fire exits. If you or an older relative are hearing-impaired, be sure there are provisions in the building's fire safety plan.

Resident-Management Relations: Who Makes the Rules?

An important thing to consider is the amount of involvement and participation in making rules and other important decisions. In some group housing, residents take responsibilities for fiscal management, property maintenance, housekeeping, rulemaking and selection of new residents. In others, sponsors handle some or all of the above, as well as counseling services, group activities, and social activities.

In general, cooperatively owned housing entails more participation, because of the vested interest residents have in common.

An interesting experiment in resident-management is being tried by Cooperative Services, Inc. (CSI), a 3,000-member consumer cooperative. Among its accomplishments are the sponsorship, development and management of 2,000 cooperative housing units in Michigan and Maryland, with another 800 currently under construction in California and Massachusetts. Funding for this housing has come from the U.S. Department of Housing and Urban Development (HUD) and from state housing authorities.

According to the general manager of CSI, CSI co-ops differ from commercial coops in that residents actually do not pay for and own the apartment or building in which they live. Rather, they pay rent, which is set at about 30% of residents' income. But tenants of CSI buildings do join CSI, the parent co-op, for a nominal fee of $100, which is refunded when the tenant leaves. Membership does not carry with it any equity interest in the apartment, the building or shares of stock. Membership does mean that residents become consumer-owners of the parent corporation, CSI, and the housing developments that are its assets. Each member has one vote in electing CSI's Board of Directors and a highly structured representative system assures that CSI is controlled and operated for the benefit of members only. Of twelve current members of the CSI Board, nine are actual co-op residents.

Within each apartment building of 150-250 units, a Building Council made up of elected representatives from each floor meets monthly with building and officers for discussion and planning. Each building has its own by-laws and remains independent as long as it operates within HUD and CSI regulations.

Budgetary management and social activities are similarly controlled by residents under this participatory-management system. CSI, the sponsor, offers interested residents educational and training programs in management skills. This saves money by having many management functions and maintenance tasks (such as landscaping and painting) performed by residents. Tenants must be in relatively good health and able to personally care for themselves to be eligible for CSI co-op living.

The Shared Housing Resource Center (SHRC) sensibly points out that autonomy and self-management are difficult ideals to implement and that not everyone wants to include them in their day-to-day living. Some would rather not have to deal with the administrative detail and personal politicking involved in self-governance, as long as the management's rules are reasonable. To others, autonomy and self-management are of primary importance and well worth the considerable effort required.

Be sure to ask questions about resident self-management when applying for any kind of senior housing. In general, housing that is controlled by a nonprofit agency most often provides some opportunity for resident participation.

Who Lives in Group Residences?

Different programs have different admissions policies with regard to residents' age, health and income. Programs sponsored by organizations receiving federal subsidies are open to people of all ethnic and religious backgrounds, as long as health and income criteria are met.

What kinds of people are drawn to different types of group living? Suprisingly, not much is known about this. Some clues, however, are provided in a 1982 study by the Shared Housing Resource Center (SHRC), of 21 shared residences of the smaller type that serve relatively independent older people.

The "typical" resident of these households was a woman in her early seventies who had resided in the group household for at least one year. The majority of the residents maintained contact with their families at least once a week (dispelling the myth that residents of shared households have been abandoned by their children or are loners). About two-thirds of the group homes were created from single-family dwellings and, interestingly, households in single homes reported fewer problems with sharing of common space than did those located in apartments, though it is unclear whether this is because of architectural features or other factors.

Monthly charges to residents varied very widely, from $50 to $1200, with varying kinds and amounts of services included in the total charge. Two-thirds of the households had some residents who received some government assistance, such as SSI or food stamps and some had experienced reductions in these benefits because of their participation in shared housing. (New legislation that will remedy this situation to a large extent is in process.) All households used community services, such as senior center programs or visiting nurses. Each household used, on the average, four such services.

Two-thirds of the households expected residents to participate at least minimally in housekeeping chores. Residents were found to have an important say in day-to-day decisions and in selection of new members, but had little input or control over other major decisions, such as hiring and firing of staff, budgetary matters and terminations of residence.

Funding for both start-up and ongoing costs was obtained from a range of sources: individuals, churches, agencies, foundations and all levels of government. After the initial renting, two-thirds of the households experienced no difficulties in recruiting new residents. A pleasant surprise was that zoning was not a problem for this group of households; neighborhood response was reported to be friendly and supportive.

This brief study gives us some insight into the accomplishments and problems experienced by some programs and their residents and provides testimony that in at least some cases, the experiment has become successfully established. The SHRC concludes that there does not seem to be one "best" model for a shared household but that each must be flexible enough in its organization to meet the mutual needs of its residents and sponsors.

Opportunities for Social Life

One of the strongest advantages offered by group housing is the opportunity for companionship, recreation and social interchange. If you or your parent are concerned about becoming isolated, having a selection of people with whom to interact may be very attractive.

Cypen Tower in Miami, Florida, is an example of senior housing in which social and recreational opportunities are the centerpiece of daily living. It was designed and built for people who are not severely ill but who are becoming increasingly frail and limited in energy. The Tower was built on the grounds of the Jewish Home and Hospital for the Aged, giving residents easy access to medical care when needed.

Cypen Tower was financed entirely with private funds—mainly by donations from philanthropic organizations. It is operated as a not-for-profit enterprise, with rental rates set to cover costs of operating only. Since Cypen Tower offers many amenities, monthly rents, which include one communal meal per day, range from $679 to $798. According to an administrator, the project aims at older people "with resources too ample for federal subsidy but short of the wealth required for residence in most for-profit facilities."

Cypen Tower is an eight-story apartment building containing 102 studio and one bedroom apartments, plus a variety of well equipped and pleasingly furnished areas devoted to social and recreational activities. The lobby includes a grand piano, a wet bar, attractive furniture and plants. A very large area is devoted to a well equipped activities and community center. All areas include special features to accommodate the frail or handicapped, such as doorways and floor surfaces suitable for safe operation of wheelchairs, waist-high electric switches, a 5-foot turning radius in bathrooms and kitchens and numerous other safety features.

Virtually all tenants pay annual dues of $12 to a tenants' organization that meets weekly with the building manager to share concerns, resolve problems and plan activities. The proximity of the hospital and nursing home enables residents with ill or institutionalized spouses to maintain frequent contact without becoming exhausted by long daily trips. By the same token, residents who fall ill can be easily visited by friends and neighbors, avoiding the isolation many hospitalized people experience.

In nearly all forms of senior housing, shared dining, laundry and recreation areas make it easy to meet people. Staff or volunteers often offer recreational activities, educational programs and trips. Residents can also take the initiative and organize social activities. In smaller group residences, people get to know one another through the business of day-to-day living. In either case, senior housing can serve to widen social horizons at a time when, for many people, this aspect of life may be especially important.

Relations with Neighborhood and Community

While few people could reasonably object to the presence of older people in their neighborhoods, the reception accorded various forms of senior housing has ranged from very cordial to somewhat cool. A cautious reception is often based on images and stereotypes associated with group living involving delinquent, mentally retarded and mentally ill people. But negative attitudes can be dispelled by good experience. One group residence reported that "after initial wariness from neighbors, the neighborhood has been delighted to see the house come into the hands of responsible owners and to have stable, long-term residents join the neighborhood."

You may find that zoning restrictions may stand in the way of establishing a group residence or larger complex. In single-family neighborhoods, variances or passage of new regulations will be necessary. But requests for variances or special permits, when well publicized, can provide opportunities for public education.

Among the many advantages to the community and neighborhod of senior housing that you can point out are:

- increased real estate taxes collected from improved and reassessed buildings;

- contributions to neighborhood revitalization when existing buildings are rehabilitated;

- increased clients for community business, industry, educational and service facilities;

- reduction or postponement of costly hospital and nursing home stays.

No concrete evidence has been produced to show that senior housing erodes property values. Existing health and social services in a given neighborhood may indeed be overtaxed by dramatic changes in the neighborhood population. But this would only apply to the case of unassisted senior housing.

If you are investigating senior housing, make sure that the plan includes provision of health and social services appropriate to your needs. Services to senior residents can be effectively coordinated if the developer has access to existing services, or is part of the community network. For example, services guaranteed to residents of New York State Enriched Housing Programs (which accommodate 350 individuals in existing housing at scattered sites) include:

- meals (residents are required to participate in at least one congregate meal per day and are assisted with other meal preparation as needed);

- housekeeping, laundry and grocery shopping;

- personal care (assistance with grooming, bathing, dressing, medicines);

- social and psychological support services;

- periodic heavy housecleaning;

- leisure activities; and

- 24-hour telephone emergency coverage.

Is Group Living For You?

To find a suitable group living arrangement for you or a relative, you will need an inquiring spirit and a good deal of first-hand contact.

These brief sketches cannot do justice to the full range of options in group housing, but they may inspire further exploration. Start with your local Area Office on Aging (see Appendix D) or with one of the groups described below.

Not all the news about senior group housing is good. The hardest fact is that there is not enough of it to meet the growing need. Senior housing was first mandated in response to a recognized need for affordable housing that would enhance independence and quality of life. The need and the mandate are still with us, though responsibility for meeting them is shifting from the public to the private sector. We can hope that in the time ahead, both sectors will make affordable housing for older Americans a top-priority issue. Those of us with the most at stake can begin to inform ourselves and to work toward that end.

To find out more about existing small group homes or how to begin, contact the Shared Housing Resource Center (SHRC), which publishes a state-by-state directory listing shared residences and group homes sponsored by nonprofit agencies. (To order, see address at the end of this chapter). In addition, SHRC offers onsite consultation and workshops to groups interested in starting a group residence anywhere and publishes a quarterly newsletter disseminating important news about developments in this field.

Another group, Action for Boston Community Development, together with Concerned Boston Citizens for Elder Affairs Housing Alternative Committee has a very helpful publication, *Planning and Developing a Shared Living Project: A Guide for Community Groups*. This guide offers practical suggestions about how to get a group residence started, choosing leaders, deciding on a plan of action, obtaining financing, selecting residents, planning living space, dealing with zoning and building codes and analyzing service needs. The complete address for obtaining this manual is also found at this chapter's end.

Key Resources

Small Group Residences

For more information about small group residences write:

Shared Housing Resource Center
6344 Greene Street
Philadelphia, PA 19144
(215) 848-1220

Besides acting as an information clearinghouse, SHRC publishes a Directory that lists, state-by-state, small group residences owned or leased by non-profit organizations. Cost: $6.00. Also available for $9.50 is a comprehensive planning manual on developing a small group residence for older people. The manual is a practical, step-by-step approach to planning, developing, financing and operation.

Action for Boston Community Development, together with the Concerned Boston Citizens for Elder Affairs, makes two planning manuals, in large print, available for $2.00 apiece. An individual planning guide for people interested in home sharing includes a sample homesharing agreement. A second community planning guide contains information about setting up small group living arrangements.

Action for Boston Community Development (ABCD)
178 Tremont Street
Boston, MA 02111
(617) 357-6000

Senior Apartments

For more information about low-cost senior apartments, we suggest calling the local Area Office on Aging (see Appendix D), the local Department of Housing (as listed in your city telephone directory) or the city/county Department of Social Services.

References

Action for Boston Community Development, *Planning and Developing a Shared Living Project: A Guide for Community Groups.* Boston, 1979.

_____, *Shared Living: Community Planning Guide.* Boston, 1982.

_____, *Shared Living: Individual Planning Guide.* Boston, 1982.

Beall, G. T., M. Thompson, et al., *Housing Older Persons in Rural America: A Handbook on Congregate Housing.* Washington, D.C.: International Center for Social Gerontology, 1981.

_____, "Federal Programs and Senior Housing," in *Housing Options for Older Americans.* Washington, D.C.: American Association of Retired Persons, 1984.

Butler, Robert, *Why Survive? Being Old in America.* New York: Harper and Row, 1975. See especially Chapter Five.

Day-Lower, Dennis, D. Bryant, et al., *National Policy Workshop on Shared Housing: Findings and Recommendations.* Philadelphia: Shared Housing Resource Center, 1982.

_____, Director, Shared Housing Resource Center, personal communication, 1983, 1984, 1985.

Haynie, William, "Cypen Tower: A Design for Retirement Living," *Aging*, January/February 1983:18-25.

Lawton, M. P., "Age and Environment," paper presented at the Tenth International Conference of Social Gerontology, Deauville, France, May 1982.

_____, "Alternative Housing," *Journal of Gerontological Social Work*, Vol. 3, Spring 1981:61-67.

Lawton, M. P., and S. Hoover, (eds.), *Community Housing Choices for the Elderly*, New York: Springer, 1981.

Leeds, Morton, "Inflation and the Elderly: A Housing Perspective," *Annals of the American Academy of Political and Social Science*, July 1980:60-69.

Lindsey, William, and B. Quint, "Elderly Services Delivery System— Ft. Lauderdale (Fla.)" *Challenge!*, U.S. Department of Housing and Urban Development, Washington, D.C., September 1980:21-24.

McElwee, E., Valuation Branch, U.S. Department of Housing and Urban Development, personal communication, August 1985.

McMahon, Martin, Director, New York State Enriched Housing Program, Albany, New York, personal communication, August 1985.

Montgomery, James, A. Stubbs, et al., "The Housing Environment of the Rural Elderly," *Gerontologist*, Vol. 20, 1980:374-81.

Myers, Phyllis, *Aging in Place: Strategies to Help the Elderly Stay in Revitalizing Neighborhoods*. Washington, D.C.: The Conservation Foundation, 1982.

New York State Department of Social Services, "Enriched Housing: A New Beginning," Albany, N. Y., n.d.

New York State Division of Housing and Community Renewal, "Shared Housing Option Program 'Shop,' " New York, n.d.

_____, " 'Shop' Fact Sheet: Answering Your Questions About the Shared Housing Option Program," Pamphlet, New York, n.d.

Olshan, Mark, Ph.D., Director, B'nai B'rith Senior Citizen Housing, personal communication, August 1984 and August 1985.

Peterson, M., Manager, Cypen Tower, Miami, Florida, personal communication, August 1985.

Potter, Joanne, Development Coordinator, Back Bay Aging Concern Committee, personal communication, August 1985.

Raglin, Harriet, Cooperative Services, Inc., personal communication, August 1985.

Sachs, Martha, "CSI: A Successful Senior Housing Cooperative," *Aging*, March/April 1983:15-18.

Shared Housing Resource Center, *National Directory of Shared Housing Programs for Older People*. Philadelphia, 1983.

_____, *Shared Housing for Older People: A Planning Manual for Group Residences*. Philadelphia, 1983.

Shared Housing Quarterly, Vol. 1, No. 1, July 1982.

Shared Housing Quarterly, Vol. 2, No. 1, March 1984.

U.S. Congress, House Select Committee on Aging, "Elderly Housing: Innovative Alternatives." Hearing before the Subcommittee on Housing and Consumer Interests, 97th Congress, first session, August 12, 1983.

U.S. Federal Register, "U.S. Department of Housing and Urban Development Section 8 Housing Assistance Payment Program, Fair Market Rent Schedules for Existing Housing and Moderate Rehabilitation," July 5, 1984, 49:27658-27714.

White House Conference on Aging, Report of the Mini-Conference on Housing for the Elderly, Washington, D.C., 1981.

White House Conference on Aging, Summary Reports of the Committee Chairmen, Washington, D.C., December 3, 1981.

Chapter 5

Retirement Communities And Life-care Plans

Retirement and life-care communities have been widely promoted as the American Dream—a return to Eden after a successful lifetime of productive work. Although only a small minority of older people can afford them, these types of living arrangements have received much media attention, contributing to the popular image of the "golden years" spent in a sun-drenched paradise.

Like most other types of group housing, retirement and life-care homes are designed for independent older people in reasonably good health. The retirement "community" may be an apartment building or complex surrounded by grounds, or it may be a "village" of single-family homes. Generally, the community is exclusively for people over a certain age—often 55—though in a very few cases, areas may be set aside for younger people and families.

Most are also intended for the relatively affluent and, therefore, include more luxury features, services, and "extras" than the forms of senior housing discussed in the last chapter. A life-care facility also guarantees personal, health, and nursing assistance. The financial relationship between residents and management may be complicated, usually involving a substantial down payment and a legal contract. Because of the cost of the investment—which may involve most of a person's total assets—and the relative permanence of these arrangements, careful research and reflection should precede any decision to enter a retirement or life-care home.

In this chapter, we will discuss retirement communities in general and life-care plans (a special type of arrangement) in particular. Although they may seem alike in some ways, the differences between them are very important.

Retirement Communities

A wide variety of housing for older people is marketed under the umbrella term "retirement community." The best examples in the field are well planned and built, soundly financed, and sensibly managed. If this lifestyle seems right for you, such a place can offer a lot of living for the money. However, many retirement communities have started out promisingly, then collapsed because of inadequate financing or inept management. And then there are examples of outright fraud and abuse, such as developers who misrepresent what they sell or fail to disclose what the real costs will be over a period of time.

Because so many retirement communities are elaborately promoted, and because regulation of this industry is sparse and erratic, excellent consumer skills plus good professional advice will be essential to make sure you get what you pay for. First, though, let's take a closer look at the specifics of retirement community life.

What Do Retirement Homes Look Like?

Most retirement communities consist of apartments or homes surrounded by grounds or acreage. The great majority are apartment buildings or complexes and are located in suburban or semirural areas. Retirees either buy or lease a living unit from a developer. Retirement communities range in size from single apartment dwellings to elaborate "villages" housing several thousand people. One group of authors who did extensive research into retirement living estimates that about half a million Americans live in fifty different retirement residences located mainly in warmer sections of the country. But this is only a rough estimate of a rapidly expanding market.

What will the new resident of a retirement community find? Retirement homes are designed to be pleasing, even impressive. Lobbies, lounges, and other public areas are attractively decorated and landscaped. Some homes offer unfurnished apartments, while others come completely furnished and equipped, down to linens, tableware, plants and art objects.

Some of these communities have central dining rooms in which one or more meals per day are served. Apartments may or may not include cooking facilities. Most often, there is access to a wide variety of indoor and outdoor recreational and social facilities: golf courses, tennis courts, swimming pools, lounges, well-equipped hobby rooms and exercise facilities. Most have graciously appointed social areas and clubrooms as well.

"Carefree living," a key selling point, is made possible by maid service, indoor and outdoor maintenance and repairs, and transportation by limousine or van to various points in the community. Private security holds down crime and helps relieve anxieties. There may be an on-site infirmary and on-duty nurse, but comprehensive medical and nursing care is not part of most retirement homes. (Of course, location near an established medical center is also a strong selling point.)

Potential for companionship and social life in a retirement home is high. As one resident noted, "People here talk to each other." Planned social events and spontaneous socializing fill a great deal of time. (In one very large Florida "retirement village," it was estimated that residents spent an average of six hours daily in planned group activity.)

Eligibility: Health and Finances

The most obvious requirement for life in a retirement community is the ability to meet the financial cost. The cost range is wide and varies according to location, type and size of housing, and services included. Estimates of monthly rentals range from $600 to $1800, according to the American Association of Homes for the Aging (AAHA). AAHA also estimates that buying into most retirement communities costs anywhere from $40,000 to $120,000. The most luxurious developments in the country cost even more.

If you are buying into a retirement community by purchasing an apartment or house, you will have to meet the same kinds of requirements demanded by any seller or mortgage lender. In addition, you will probably be paying monthly maintenance fees, plus yearly owners' association dues. If you rent, as most retirement-home residents do, maintenance costs may be reflected in your rental payment or may be added on. Whether you rent or buy, you may also have to pay a nonrefundable entrance fee.

The retirement-home administration may ask for proof of income continuity, even if the purchaser is paying cash for the unit. What the management wants is assurance that the buyer will have enough disposable income and insurance to pay for future maintenance, health care expenses and other costs of living.

Most homes require applicants to be in generally good health or, at the very least, ambulatory at time of entrance. Other, more subtle social criteria may also operate. While retirement communities do not overtly use race, religion, or social class as a basis for entry, a great many tend to attract very similar kinds of people. If you are interested in a particular community, it is helpful to learn something about the people who will be your co-residents and neighbors, and to decide if they are a compatible group for you.

Resident-Management Relations

Relationship with management depends at least partly on whether you own or rent your living unit. Ownership involves more than just sharing expenses for the upkeep and maintenance of your individual unit and its surroundings. Many retirement communities have a residents' association or owners' association that deals with management on a range of issues that affect the whole community, such as planned physical changes, admission of new applicants, and fiscal management.

You might want to become involved in such a group. But should you decide to leave planning and decision-making to others, make sure that residents' association members are qualified to deal with legal, financial, and human relations problems. Their decisions will affect your life. You should also be clear about the differences between condominium and cooperative ownership. In a condominium, you own the apartment or house and the land it stands on. In a co-op, you own a share in the total property, along with all the other co-op members. Home and condominium ownership generally mean more individual control over the property and the ability to make decisions affecting it on your own. Co-op ownership means more involvement in group decision-making.

Relationships with the Wider Community

Relations between a retirement community and its surrounding neighborhood can vary widely. Some communities blend into their neighborhoods; they may even reach out to area residents by opening up activities and facilities to older people living nearby. Others are walled off from their surroundings or geographically isolated from the nearest cities and towns.

Most retirement communities are for older people only, so it is important to consider how you will feel about living exclusively with people your own age. Many analysts of retirement living think it unwise for older people to segregate themselves from younger people. (From this viewpoint, retirement homes have even been called "traps.") A smaller number of professionals take the opposite view— that it is natural and healthy for older people to seek the company of their peers and to protect themselves from crime, noise, dirt and other unpleasant features of modern urban life.

Whatever the experts may say, it is very important to find out beforehand how open to the surrounding community a given retirement home may be, and to be certain that this meshes with your needs, as you see them at this point in your life.

Most neighborhoods react positively to retirement communities in their midst. Retirement residences tend to be located in well-kept areas and to be well maintained. While contributing to the community tax base, they place little strain on such community resources as schools and welfare agencies. For these reasons alone they should be very welcome. It should be noted, though, that some retirees say they perceive a cool attitude on the part of their immediate communities. You may want to ask about this when you visit.

Pros and Cons of Retirement-Community Life

Retirement-community living is not for everyone, not even for everyone who can afford it, yet most older Americans, when questioned, say they would like to live in a retirement community, despite the fact that social scientists contend that this is not the best choice for them. What exactly are the pros and cons? You might be interested in the results of a survey on this subject that involved 1400 residents of retirement communities.

Not surprisingly, most people who have already chosen this way of life express satisfaction with their choice. Retirement communities seem to appeal to several kinds of people. They are attractive to the adventurous—those who are willing to pull up stakes and move to a new place, among new people. (Remember that in the retirement community, strangers do not stay strangers long.) They appeal to people who feel isolated—many of their friends and relatives have moved away or died, and the retirement community offers a whole new area for social contacts. They are of interest to those who have health and energy problems that are beginning to impose limits on their lives, and the availability of everything people need within a small community can help them keep psychologically and physically fit.

Among the 1,400 people who responded to a questionnaire about their experiences, the following advantages were mentioned most frequently:

- community spirit and sense of belonging; ease in meeting people; built-in opportunities for social life;

- on-site recreational and athletic facilities;

- convenient, worry-free living; easy access to services;

- cleanliness, peacefulness; well-ordered daily life;

- security from crime and fear of crime;

- financial appreciation in the value of home or apartment.

A minority who tried retirement-home life and were dissatisfied listed the following as reasons for disillusionment. These reasons deserve attention, because most of them were also mentioned by those who were, on the whole, satisfied with their lives:

- rising cost of initial purchase and monthly maintenance fees; middle-income people priced out of the market;

- overcrowding (one large Arizona retirement village grew to more than 50,000 by 1981, with another 75,000 people projected to enter during the 1980s);

- too much similarity in age, religion, ethnic background and attitudes among residents;

- uniformity and narrowness of outlook and interests among fellow residents;

- overregulation of daily life; too much organization;

- inadequate privacy;

- unfair distribution of costs (special facilities, such as golf course and tennis courts, add to costs for nonusers);

- remoteness from cultural and commercial centers;

- depressing effects of age segregation; repeated exposure to illness, deaths, losses.

A choice of this or any other lifestyle comes down to a tradeoff between benefits and the price you must pay for them. For some people, the balance between advantages and disadvantages may be very clearly weighted in one direction. For others, it is a close contest, requiring further investigation and perhaps an experimental trial period. Whether definitely interested or still not quite sure, you will want to read on about how to shop carefully for a retirement home.

Shopping For a Retirement Residence

The first objective is to consult with a qualified professional who works for you. Admittedly, it is not easy to find a lawyer, accountant, or financial consultant who is thoroughly knowledgeable in this field. You may have to spend some time looking for an adviser before you shop for a retirement community. But because of the high level of investment, it is worth taking the extra time.

Do not accept a real estate agent, a representative of the retirement community or their lawyer as an adviser. No matter how well informed or helpful these people may be, they are working for their employers, not for you. There is certainly no reason why you shouldn't initiate contact with a developer, ask questions, and pay a visit to the site to inspect it and make sure it is what you want. If you have already proceeded further than this on your own, do not sign anything without reviewing the contract and the entire situation with an informed adviser whom you have hired for this specific task.

In gathering initial information, don't hesitate to ask questions about the reputation of the builder or developer and the management. Don't rely solely on information from your friends who have already bought into the retirement home. Their opinion is valuable in terms of providing an inside look at many aspects of life in the home and they can also inform you about problems. But don't assume that just because your friends are satisfied, you will be too. Every contract is an individual transaction, and retirement homes are part of a business that experiences day-to-day fluctuations in operation.

As you shop, it is essential to understand fully your present and future financial costs. Some costs are obvious; others may be hidden. Marika Sumichrast, a former vice president of marketing and sales with a large retirement community, outlines an excellent checklist. To begin with, she says, you should always assume that retirement-living costs will be more than the management estimates. If you are buying, here are some important questions to ask in regard to costs:

1.   **The entrance fee:** Most retirement communities have one, and it is usually nonrefundable. How much is it, and is it likely to increase between now and the time you buy? Sumichrast recommends adding 10 to 20 percent to the stated estimate, to take in extra or last-minute changes.

2.   **The sale price:** Be sure it is fair. Is it comparable to similar housing available in the same geographic area? A difference of no more than 5 to 10 percent is reasonable, because of special features in housing for older people.

3.   **Appreciation:** Is it likely to be consistent with appreciation on similar housing in the same area? Examine past and present sales in the community through a realtor or in the public record.

4. **The mortgage:** What will you pay each month? Is the interest rate fixed or variable? If the latter, can you afford a higher rate than the initial one? Is there a cap on the variable mortgage rate, and will you be able to meet it?

5. **Taxes and insurance:** Remember that you will need enough money to cover homeowners' insurance and all applicable taxes. Find out about all the taxes you will be responsible for (school tax, sewer tax, etc.) and be sure to compute them into your estimate of monthly housing costs.

6. **Maintenance charges and homeowners' association dues:** Besides your mortgage, taxes and insurance, you should expect to pay some maintenance costs—for example, general repairs, owners' association fees, and water assessments. Find out exactly which ones you have to pay and how much the charges will be.

7. **Energy efficiency:** Sumichrast says, "Insist on knowing the insulation value [sometimes called the R-value], type of windows and doors, and costs of utilities." Then ask a local builder what is appropriate for the area. Poor insulation can produce huge heating and air conditioning bills.

If you are buying a lot (or a house and lot) in a subdivision, make sure the lot is served by water and sewer systems, paved roads, electricity, and phone lines. If it is not, find out what it will cost to install the necessary facilities and decide if your finances will allow these costs. You also need to know if enough water is guaranteed to supply the entire subdivision when it is fully occupied. These points are especially important if you are a city dweller and unaccustomed to concerning yourself with such necessities. Many Easterners are surprised to find that in many parts of the Sunbelt water is so scarce that there is a charge for every drop! It is never wise to buy any land sight unseen, no matter how seductive the pictures or the financial terms.

Personal factors are as important as financial ones in deciding whether a retirement home is a good investment for you. You need to think not only about what appeals to you at the moment but also what might become important to you in the foreseeable future. For instance, many people entering the retirement stage of life are glad to be free from the burden of meal preparation and cleanup, and therefore choose accommodations that include no kitchen facilities. Sumichrast and others advise against buying units that lack some kitchen and eating space, because in their survey they found that many people regretted this choice, once the novelty of not preparing meals wore off.

Among the many personal factors to be weighed, probably the most important is whether living exclusively with other people your age appeals to you. You might try and envision what the community will be like in twenty years. If present residents are in their sixties, and over the years they are not replaced by younger members, will the community continue to function efficiently when all residents are in their eighties?

A last word of advice: never buy without first visiting and viewing an actual model, whether you are purchasing a detached home, a condominium, or a co-op. Many sales are made before completion of the actual unit or building takes place. Heed this advice from Ms. Sumichrast: "Insist on inspection at least two weeks before settlement. Make a list of any needed work. Go back again before settlement to see whether the work was done. Never go to settlement without all items being taken care of to your satisfaction."

The American Association of Housing for the Aging (AAHA) emphasizes the importance of making sure that any payment for space in yet-to-be constructed buildings is held in escrow or otherwise protected until construction is completed. AAHA also states that a full refund should be available to any consumer who pays in advance on an unconstructed retirement home and decides at a later point not to go ahead with the purchase. It is important that assurance of refundability be stated in writing.

Even if you and other members of your family have been thorough and thoughtful in going through all these steps, do not sign a contract until you have reviewed all agreements with an administrator (not a salesperson) for the community and with your own lawyer or adviser.

If you do not presently have a lawyer, look in the phone book for the Information and Referral phone number of your city or county government and request referral to a source of legal assistance. If no I&R number is listed, call any of the organizations representing the interests of older people listed in the back of this book. Investment in a retirement residence ties up the major part of the capital most older people have at their disposal. The only housing decision calling for equal caution is the decision to invest your funds in a life-care community, the next topic in this chapter.

Life-Care Plans

Outwardly, life-care communities may look just like the retirement communities we just described. But they are different in two very important ways.

First, residents of a life-care community seldom own or have equity in their living units, even though a substantial entrance payment is involved.

Second, the typical life-care contract guarantees, along with lifetime occupancy of the unit (contingent on paying a monthly fee), specified health and nursing care you may later require. The chief commodity you purchase in a life-care community is security—the assurance of lifetime shelter and care.

Life-care communities (or continuing-care homes, as they are occasionally called) are a recent entry on the American housing scene. Originally, they were sponsored by nonprofit organizations such as churches and fraternal groups, but recently private developers have recognized their market potential. During 1985-89, the Marriott Corporation, for example, will build three new life-care communities housing three to four hundred people each in the Washington, D.C., area and elsewhere, according to *The Washington Post. The Wall Street Journal* reports that the selling of life-care apartments is considered by the new industry to be at least as lucrative as the selling of condominiums. The National Consumers League cites an estimate by the U.S. Senate Special Committee on Aging that a third of all life-care plans now operate for profit, with annual revenues estimated at about $1 billion.

Because life-care homes are a rapidly growing enterprise and because they are not regulated, little is known about their numbers. The U.S. Senate Special Committee on Aging calculates roughly that between four to six hundred are operating nationally, housing an estimated 100,000 people.

Financial Features of Life-Care Plans

As we discussed earlier, to enter a life-care home you will have to make a substantial lump-sum entry payment plus monthly payments. In return, you receive the right to lifetime occupancy and a specific package of nursing care, when and if it is needed.

Some early plans required residents to turn over their assets in full. Fortunately, this arrangement has fallen into disuse. It is much too risky for residents and not really a fair exchange of value. If you come across a developer who wants you to sign over your assets in full, look elsewhere.

Some life-care contracts operate on a pay-as-you-go basis. In exchange for a permanent lease, residents pay a monthly fee in addition to personal health costs as these may occur. This is not a true life-care plan, since no health and nursing services are guaranteed. There is nothing wrong with the plan per se, except that you may be confronted with large, unexpected medical expenses as the years progress and be unable to keep up your monthly payments. If you are interested in a home offering such an arrangement, you should not have to pay as large an entry fee as you would pay to a home that includes health-care services. Do some comparative shopping!

The most frequent arrangement is one in which you pay an entrance fee, plus monthly fees (which may be subject to change) for as long as you live. In a soundly operated life-care community, the lump-sum entry fee usually goes toward the home's repayment of its major capital expenses, while the monthly fees cover ongoing operating costs. You can expect the entry fee to be substantial—fees of $20,000 to $200,000 have been reported, with the average fee estimated at about $35,000. Monthly fees average several hundred dollars per person, not per couple! You may receive a partial refund of the entry fee if you decide to leave the community within a few years after you join. Otherwise, this fee is generally nonrefundable. So it's extremely important, if you choose a life-care plan, to be absolutely certain that this is the way you want to live your future years.

In order to maintain quality property and services in a fluctuating economy, the home must expect to make financial adjustments over time. This means that residents should expect periodic increases in the monthly fee. Increases should be reasonable; that is, they should be tied to cost-of-living increases or some other economic index. Ask about past increases. Ask if there is a cap on how high the monthly payment can go. Beware of plans that guarantee no monthly increases; this will almost certainly result in curtailment of promised services, diminished quality, or, in the extreme case, bankruptcy. Remember that your financial security will depend on the home's solvency, once you are a resident. Continuing care is a mutual commitment.

Range of Services Provided

Aside from its health-care package, the services provided by life-care communities are essentially the same as those described for retirement residences earlier in the chapter. In addition to meal and maid service, maintenance, repairs, transportation, security, recreational, educational, and social activities, some homes may also offer counseling and social services relevant to problems encountered by older adults (illness, widowhood, separation from extended family). Some also cover funeral costs as part of the contract.

Resident-Management Relations

About two-thirds of all life-care homes are sponsored by nonprofit organizations, such as a churches, civic organizations or trade unions. These sponsors may have a moral commitment to the home, but are seldom legally responsible for the home's financial situation or its day-to-day management. In some cases, the civic group or religious denomination whose name appears in the home's title has little or nothing to do with the home. Typically, management is subcontracted to a commercial or nonprofit management firm, which deals directly with residents or with a residents' association.

Many nonprofit homes also have boards of directors, drawn from the local community. Some boards are merely figureheads, while others are empowered to establish policies for the home. If you are interested in a nonprofit-sponsored home, find out who is on the board and what power the board has to make decisions affecting your future. If the philosophy of the board is in serious conflict with your own on the way you would like to lead your personal life, this may not be the right place for you. Dress codes and rules for male-female behavior may not seem important at the time you are planning for such basics as health and finances, but they will affect the quality of your life and overall satisfaction with the choice you make.

Eligibility: Health and Finances

Life-care communities have an even stronger stake than retirement residences in your health and financial status. If you apply, you will be asked for a great deal of financial disclosure and will undergo a thorough medical examination. To operate a life-care plan on a sound basis and to deliver the promised services, management must screen applicants on the basis of strict standards.

Don't assume, however, that if you have ever been ill or hospitalized, you will be automatically disqualified. Decisions are made on an actuarial basis—on the percentages—and every organization takes some calculated risks.

The purpose of financial disclosure is to assure that, in the opinion of the management, you will be able to meet rising monthly payments and that you will have enough money left to pay for normal living expenses and incidentals not covered by the home. Terminations are not good for public relations, and, of course, they can be devastating to the individuals concerned.

Don't attempt to keep secret anything relating to your health or finances. If the discrepancy is discovered, your contract with the home may be invalidated, to your disadvantage. And remember—examination of your health and finances doesn't take place until after you make formal application. So, if the idea of a life-care community appeals to you, do not be deterred from making inquiries and collecting information.

Your Relations with the Local Community

Retirement and life-care homes are usually regarded as desirable members of the neighborhoods in which they are situated. Local newspapers often contain reports of educational and social events taking place at the community or about the accomplishments of individual members. This is good publicity for the home and can help dispel some myths and stereotypes about older people that continue to circulate. In addition, the influx of a relatively affluent group of consumers into any area is a boon to local merchants and providers of services.

The Washington Post recently described how one couple made the decision to enter a life-care community:

"Raking the lawn and cleaning the gutters just got to be too much," says William Mason, a retired District of Columbia government supervisor. "We didn't want to be a burden to anyone, but we wanted to live someplace where we could get care for the rest of our lives." So the 74-year-old Mason and his 79-year-old wife, Faith, sold their Rockville house and paid an entrance fee of $76,000 and now pay monthly fees of $1,655 to live in Goodwin House in Alexandria. For their money, the Masons can have three meals a day in communal dining, housekeeping, some health services, apartment maintenance and repairs and a program of activities and trips with the three hundred others living in the same high-rise. If the Masons can no longer function independently, they can move into the Goodwin House health-care center, where, for basically no extra cost, they can receive nursing care. "When you get to be our age, you have the feeling that something could happen at any time. Here we know we can be taken care of immediately," says Mason, who found out how quick that help could be several months ago, when he suffered chest pains. A nurse arrived within seconds after he pushed a call button in his apartment. "If I'd been in a regular apartment building, I would have waited a long time for that help."

Pros and Cons of Life-Care Living

Entering a life-care community is obviously a good move for some people. The question is, will it be right for you? Before making a decision, you should analyze all the factors involved in retirement residences and, perhaps, review the advantages and disadvantages of retirement communities discussed earlier in this chapter.

A decision to contract for life care is especially serious because of the relative permanence of the arrangement. Again, withdrawing from a life care contract is possible but difficult, and almost always involves a substantial financial penalty.

To make things even more complicated, it is difficult to determine whether or not a contract you sign today will be advantageous five, ten, or twenty years in the future. You need to feel especially secure about the ability to pay the costs later on. To make the right choice, this creates the need for some good, investigative work on your part, as well as sound professional advice and consultation. If you think a life-care community is where you might like to spend the rest of your years, the work may be well worth it.

Shopping for a Life-Care Community: How to Begin

The research job may seem formidable, but it can be made more manageable by taking one step at a time. We suggest you start by calculating your own financial prospects, using the Estimated Monthly Income Chart and the Total Assets and Net Worth Chart in Chapter One, if you haven't already done so. The value of completing this first step is that you don't waste time investigating and visiting a residence you cannot possibly afford.

Or, you may prefer to begin at your local library or bookstore with one of several existing directories to life-care communities. Look under the geographic areas that interest you and, using the descriptions in the directory, check off homes that appear promising.

At this stage, you can use the phone to eliminate possibilities that don't match well with your needs. Now you are ready to write to the homes that meet your standards and needs, requesting descriptive materials. While waiting for the return mail, if you have not done so already, fill out the financial charts in Chapter One. You'll find them helpful in evaluating the materials you receive.

The American Association of Homes for the Aging (AAHA), which represents the nonprofit sector of the retirement-home industry, lists some basic questions that a person interested in applying should ask. Some may be answered by the descriptive materials sent to you or by the home's handbook of rules. Never sign any contract until all the questions you have in all the following categories have been answered satisfactorily, in reasonable detail and in writing:

- how will you pay for shelter and care?
- who is responsible for the home and its actions?
- what is the home's financial condition?
- how is the home administered?
- what living units and services are provided?
- what health and nursing care is provided?

- what are its discharge and transfer policies?

- what refunds and fee adjustments are guaranteed?

You can organize these questions by listing each item on the left-hand side of a large sheet of paper and creating an answer column to the right. As you write and telephone, use one sheet for each home you contact. Add more questions that occur to you as a result of these early conversations. (You may want to file these and other materials in a looseleaf notebook.)

If you are interested in one or more homes located close to where you live, it is a good idea to pay a visit, once you've written, telephoned, and organized your financial charts. Take your question list with you. Even if you don't like the place when you visit, you will learn a lot about retirement living and be better able to decide what you do and don't like about it. If the home is some distance away, you can continue your contacts by telephone or through written communication before arranging a visit. By visiting and dealing with a number of retirement/life-care communities, you gain knowledge and skills that will make your eventual decision a sound one.

It makes sense to inquire about eligibility for entrance before arranging a visit. Does the home have any restrictive policies about age, sex, health, religious affiliation, economic resources, marital status? While it is an excellent idea to visit a few different homes for the sake of comparison, you won't want to waste time on homes with restrictive policies that make you uncomfortable.

If you do not already have a written copy of the home's rules and regulations, ask for one to be sent before your visit. Take time to look through the handbook, and delete and add to your own question list. It is important to do this in a calm, unpressured atmosphere. Once you arrive for a visit, there will be a great number of new impressions that can distract you. So read, reflect, and formulate your questions beforehand.

The American Association of Housing for the Aging (AAHA) advises that your visit include discussion of the home's operating policies and rules with admissions staff (not with salespersons). While visiting, you should also ask for an explanation of how the home's rules and policies are established. Do residents participate in decisions affecting daily life? What is the nature of participation? Is there a residents' association, and how active is it?

Serious Shopping

Let's suppose that you have done some preliminary research on life-care communities and are fairly convinced that this could be a good way of life for you. By now you should have a file of materials and many notes from phone conversations. You've probably visited two or three homes in your vicinity and perhaps one or two in more distant places. It is now a matter of comparing the places you have narrowed down. Or, perhaps you have a specific place in mind and want as many details as possible so you might begin negotiating. The following section will help to guide you through this more serious stage of events.

You are the customer in a highly competitive business. The stringent health and financial entrance requirements make some people feel intimidated, as though they are applying for membership in an exclusive club, not a life-care community. But life-care communities are an industry, selling a product, and you are the consumer.

A good consumer is never too embarrassed to ask questions, to request proof of claims in writing, and to negotiate the most advantageous terms possible. If you assert yourself in a courteous but firm manner and receive evasive replies or the implication that your questions are insulting, beware! Inform the representative that the investment you are making requires written assurances.

A truly reputable, soundly run operation will comply with your requests and not try to discourage them with statements about trust, good faith or the home's religious sponsorship. (Remember that religious or other sponsoring organizations rarely have legal responsibility for the financial condition or business operations of the home.) If in doubt, inform the representative that you will discuss matters with your banker or lawyer and contact the company within a reasonable period of time. Never let anyone persuade you to sign a contract before you have all the facts, because you might lose your place on a waiting list.

Of course, you cannot postpone the decision indefinitely. Following are the important final questions you will need answered before signing a contract.

Finances: Theirs and Yours

Whether or not you can handle the costs of a life care home depends on the home's financial condition as much as your own. Yet these are some of the questions many people hesitate to ask. These are vital questions. Ask them. If the home goes into bankruptcy (and some have), the results will be disastrous for residents, who may be left virtually destitute. Cover all the following points and be certain to obtain written documentation for each one.

It is essential that you know the source of the home's revenues and how those revenues are spent. If the home is a new one, with no established track record, a banker, accountant or other financial adviser that you have engaged for this should help evaluate the financial health of company. The representative of the life care community should provide you with a copy of an audited financial statement; if they fail to do so, ask for one. Make sure the statement includes a declaration that it has been prepared in conformity with "accepted accounting principles." If this important phrase is missing, be very skeptical about the information contained in the financial statement and hire a reputable accountant to go over the statement and interpret it with you.

It is also necessary to know how the home uses or invests the lump-sum entrance payments it receives. Is this money used to construct new facilities, to improve existing ones, to provide continuing health care, to pay day-to-day operating costs? Experts agree that the soundest operation is one in which lump-sum entrance fees are used to pay off the home's long-term obligations and monthly fees are used to cover operating costs. Beware of a home that uses some or all of the entrance fee to cover its day-to-day expenses.

Ask about the home's financial history. Has it ever operated at a loss? How was the loss made up? Have there been any bankruptcies? Losses and bankruptcies in the past should not disqualify the home from consideration, provided, of course, that it is now under sound financial management and operating in the black.

Ask whether reserves are specifically earmarked for residents' future health-care needs. A newly established life-care community usually admits only healthy people. In the future, a number of these individuals may require nursing care, which can be a very expensive proposition. Unless the management has established a health-care reserve in anticipation of this, monthly fees will increase at a rate greater than the inflation rate, so that the promised care can be provided.

Finally, you should ask about financial and legal relationships with the home's sponsors. What are the sponsor's responsibilities to the home, its residents, and its creditors? What are their specific commitments in case of financial problems? What is the home's relationship with the commercial lending institution holding the mortgage? What is the history of the mortgage?

Ask for written evidence of all credentials (such as church sponsorships) and linkages to any nonprofit or governmental agencies. Accept only direct documentation from the home. Do not accept any statements contained in advertisements, publicity materials, or newspaper stories. Do not accept statements in the brochures or pamphlets published by the home—they are not legally binding. Again, if representatives of the home take offense at your requests for documentation, you should exercise extreme caution. The potential for fraud and abuse in this industry is present and will be discussed in more detail further on.

A general book, such as this one, cannot offer specific advice about your financial situation. That is one of the reasons why it is so important that you use a professional consultant. We can point out some questions on which most consumers will probably need to focus. Once you have determined that the life-care community you are considering is a sound investment, you will need to calculate whether you can meet anticipated future costs without undue strain.

If a particular home is too expensive, don't give up on it if you are really interested in this lifestyle, especially if the margin of difference is small. Costs vary from place to place and one region to another. Investigate a different home in a different location and compare. You will want to ask yourself the following questions about any home in any location:

- Are the charges comparable and competitive with similar types of homes offering similar services in the same geographic area? How much of a premium are you willing to pay for climate? For proximity to family?

- Does the home have more than one method of payment? Are they willing to work out a variation that fits your needs and to make the adjustment legally binding?

- If the home requires any payment prior to occupancy, (other than the cost of processing the application) is that payment refundable? This can be important if you decide to make simultaneous applications.

Experts in the retirement field advise that you should count on costs exceeding what the retirement or life-care home predicts by about 5 to 10 percent. In a well-run home, you should count on periodic increases in monthly fees. It is very difficult to anticipate the extent of these increases, but you can ask the home if there is a cap and what the cap is. Ask for a guarantee in writing; verbal promises are usually impossible to enforce.

Your present age and health will also influence any decision you make concerning the affordability of a life care home. Dipping into capital when you are a hale and healthy 65 is generally considered dangerous; at 80 or 85, it might be worth reconsidering. We cannot say too often that it is essential to have professional advice when you are making decisions about an investment as large and important as this one.

We have paid a lot of attention to finances because of their importance to most people. But there are other aspects of living about which you will want to be equally well informed and careful.

Medical and nursing care
Next to finances, this will be a critical issue for most entrants into life-care plans. Even if you and your spouse are perfectly healthy now and expect to live to 100, responsible planning must include the possibility that one or both of you may require medical attention and nursing or personal care in the future. This issue is even more crucial for people who discontinue their insurance, under the assumption that the home and Medicare, between them, will take care of all contingencies.

While most life-care homes accept Medicare, Medicare only covers limited amounts of hospital care, very short-term nursing, and personal care under certain circumstances. It does not cover medication, eyeglasses, and other items.

You must find out which medical and nursing services are covered by your life-care contract. List each of the following services on your question sheet, under medical and nursing care, checking off those items that are included in your contract:

- physicians' services;
- skilled nursing care on or off the premises;
- personal care;

- inpatient hospital care;

- outpatient hospital procedures and treatments;

- dental care;

- rehabilitative services, including physical therapy, occupational therapy, speech therapy;

- emergency treatment, with a doctor on call;

- ambulance service;

- eyeglasses, hearing aids;

- medicines and other non-Medicare items.

Now find out which of the unchecked items on the list are covered or co-insured by a health insurance policy you plan to keep. Make sure you have adequate financial resources for dealing with expenses that do not fall in either category.

It is important to know not only the items covered, but what the ceilings and limitations are on each. If you believe you will travel after you enter the home, find out about coverage for any expenses incurred while you are elsewhere. Of the above expenses, those that are not covered by your contract and Medicare in tandem must be calculated into your own budget over the long term.

Specifics about services

Ideally, all services offered by the home should be spelled out in the contract. If anything is not, ask for a written memo or rider to the contract specifying what those services will be. Don't accept a general description, such as "maid service." You need to know how often and for how many hours each time maid service is provided. What jobs are included?

If you have individual needs that are not specifically addressed in the contract, discuss and have them included in writing before closing your deal. If those needs are important, make sure they will be available to you as a matter of contract, and not as "favor."

Rules for daily living

If you have received a handbook and discussed the home's rules and regulations during an early contact or visit, by now you will probably be well informed about them. If you have not examined or discussed them, now is the time. The rules and regulations will be crucial to the quality of life you experience once you are a member of the community.

Make sure you can live comfortably with the philosophy of the home's sponsors and with their views of propriety and morality. (For example, certain homes regulate relations between men and women residents by prohibiting visits in residents' rooms.) In other instances, rules are informally imposed by expressions of disapproval. Make certain the rules are consistent with the way you wish to live and that there aren't so many that they interfere with living. You are probably accustomed to making your own decisions, but remember that you do not own the unit you occupy in the home: you are leasing it from an organization with its own objectives and philosophy.

If you are in serious doubt about any of the rules, find out what powers the board of directors has in making and enforcing policy. Find out also who is on the board and what roles they play in the general community. You will have to decide on the basis of what you learn whether you will be comfortable living with the rules and regulations of that particular group and whether or not the rules and regulations will interfere with your personal freedom.

Widow(er)hood and Life-Care
If you or your relative is single, divorced, separated, or widowed at the time of application your status as an individual contractee will remain unchanged (unless, of course, you marry while you are a resident). If you are applying as a couple, then you need to know what will happen to the survivor should one partner die.

All agreements about the rights of a surviving spouse should be explicitly stated in the contract. It is reasonable to insist on continuing life care for the survivor. Some homes, in fact, will reduce the monthly rate for the surviving resident to the rate currently paid by single applicants. In other homes, a surviving spouse must occupy a smaller unit than he or she occupied as part of a couple. You will also want to know the home's policy on returning unused fees to the estate of a deceased resident and how funeral expenses are covered.

Terminating Relations
Your relationship to the life-care community may be ended by voluntary withdrawal or prolonged absence on your part, by failure to pay monthly maintenance fees, or by death. You will want to be very clear in advance about how each of these circumstances will be handled.

The home's handbook should contain a clear statement of its discharge policies which should spell out the circumstances warranting discharge and who is to be involved in the decision. Your contract should specify whether any unused part of the entrance fee is to be refunded in case of discharge by the home, or if changed circumstances lead you to voluntarily withdraw.

Fraud and Mismanagement: How to Avoid Them

It is probable that many or most life-care communities conduct business in a principled manner and are reasonably well managed. But some have been shown to be badly lacking on both counts. Nor are the bad examples confined to the commercial sector of the industry; in fact, the difference between for-profit and not-for-profit is blurred because many homes are sponsored by one organization, owned by another, and promoted and managed by yet a third.

The potential for fraud and mismanagement is enhanced by the lack of federal regulation or consumer protection in the life-care industry. As of this writing, only eleven states require some regulation, accreditation, or other form of consumer protection relating to life-care homes. Those states are: Arizona, California, Colorado, Florida, Illinois, Indiana, Maryland, Michigan, Minnesota, Missouri, and Pennsylvania.

Because of the lack of consistent standards, the industry has a very uneven performance record. The record includes cases of intentional fraud as well as cases of unintentional mismanagement leading to financial failure. An example of the latter is Pacific Homes, a California-based nonprofit agency that managed fourteen communities and went bankrupt in 1979. The homes had some 2,000 residents. In case of bankruptcy, residents receive no refunds, and are, in effect, homeless. For those living in a life-care community, the results of deliberate fraud and unintended failure are, of course, equally disastrous.

Despite the lack of regulation, the individual consumer does not stand completely alone. The U.S. Federal Trade Commission (FTC) has been active in investigating individual cases and issuing orders restraining the activities of industry abusers. Private groups such as the National Consumers League, the American Association of

Retired Persons, the American Association of Homes for the Aging, and Consumers Union have engaged in public education on the subject of life-care communities. And AAHA has begun organizing a national accreditation commission, which is expected to start functioning in 1986.

But for now, if you are seriously interested in entering a life-care community, what can you as an individual do to protect yourself against fraud, abuse or unreasonable risk? Virtually all of the problems uncovered by the FTC lay in the area of inadequate or false disclosure by the company concerning its own financial condition and risks to residents. By following the procedures outlined in this chapter—investigating thoroughly, obtaining written documentation and consulting with professionals you can guard effectively against fraud or incompetence.

The National Consumers League emphasizes that the main commodity you buy when you contract for life care is security against isolation. "The combined costs of shelter, food, health care, and other services will probably be higher than if you purchased them in the general community. Security comes at a premium, but your job is to make sure the premium is not excessive, in terms of your own values and priorities. All ventures involve some risk, but you can minimize those risks by exercising your responsibilities and rights as a consumer, with the best help available to you.

Key Resources

Retirement Communities

The Public Affairs Committee publishes pamphlets for the public on various issues, including living arrangements for older Americans. Write:

The Public Affairs Committee
381 Park Avenue South
New York, NY 10016

If you are thinking about purchasing a home or land in a planned development, a useful booklet is "The Insiders Guide to Owning

Land in Subdivisions," available from INFORM for $2.50, plus 71¢ postage and handling. Write:

INFORM
381 Park Avenue South
New York, New York 10016
(212) 689-4040

Life Care Communities

The National Consumers League publishes a pamphlet entitled, "A Consumer Guide to Life Care Communities," available for $3.00. Write:

National Consumers League
600 Maryland Avenue, SW
202 West Wing
Washington, DC 20024
(202) 554-1600

A useful book entitled *National Continuing Care Directory* is available from AARP Books for $13.95 ($1.45 postage and handling). Write:

American Association for Retired Persons
Books Department CATA
400 South Edward Street
Mt. Prospect, IL 60056

Note: No phone orders are accepted.

References

American Association of Homes for the Aging, *Continuing Care Homes: A Guidebook for Consumers*. Washington, D.C., 1976.

_____, *The Continuing Care Retirement Community*, brochure, n.d.

_____, *Planning Housing and Services for the Elderly; Guidebook No. 102*. Washington, D.C., 1977.

_____, *Resident Decision-Making in Homes for the Aging*. Washington, D.C., 1982.

_____, Program Announcement, 23rd Annual Meeting, 1984.

Baldwin, Leo, "Retirement Communities," in *Housing Options for Older Americans*. Washington, D.C.: American Association of Retired Persons, 1984.

Collins, Glen, "Many More Elderly Migrate to New States," *New York Times*, December 19, 1983.

Dickman, Irving, and M. Dickman, "Where Older People Live: Living Arrangements for the Elderly," New York City Bureau of Public Affairs, Pamphlet No. 556, n.d.

Haught, Evelyn, Director of Public Relations, American Association of Homes for the Aging, personal communication, August 1985.

"Interest in Congregate Housing Grows," *Wall Street Journal*, November 17, 1982.

Lifecare Industry: 4th Annual Report on the Lifecare Industry in the U.S. Philadelphia: Laventhol & Horwath, 1984.

Laventhol & Horwath, "Entrepreneurs Entering Lifecare Retirement Field Means Intense Competition," news release, n.d.

Lehman, Virginia, *You, the Law and Retirement*, U.S. Department of Health, Education and Welfare, Administration on Aging, Washington, D.C., 1973.

Life Care Society of America, Inc., *Consumers Guide to Independent Living for Older Americans: The Life Care Alternative*. Doylestown, PA., 1979.

National Consumers League, "Consumers Guide to Life Care Communities," pamphlet, 1984.

Nelson, Thomas, *Consumer Problems of the Elderly*. Washington, D.C.: U.S. Department of Commerce, National Technical Information Service, 1978.

Ross, Eric, Staff Builders Home Health Care, Inc., personal communication, August 1985.

Simko, Patricia, *The Insider's Guide to Owning Land in Subdivisions*. New York: INFORM, 1980.

Southern California Presbyterian Homes, *Annual Report 1982-83*. Glendale, Calif., 1983.

———, "By This We Live," guidelines, n.d.

———, brochure, n.d.

Sullivan, Marguerite, "The Pursuit of Continuing Care," *Washington Post*, November 30, 1984.

Sumichrast, M., R. Shafer, and M. Sumichrast, *Planning Your Retirement Housing*. Glenview, Ill: AARP Books, Scott, Foresman and Company, 1984.

United States of America, before Federal Trade Commission, File No. 782 3081, Agreement Containing Consent Order to Cease and Desist in the Matter of Christian Services International, Inc., March 1, 1983.

U.S. Federal Trade Commission, *News Notes*, May 1983.

U.S. Health Care Financing Administration, *Medicare Reference Chart*, 1985.

U.S. Senate, testimony of Commissioner Patricia P. Bailey concerning Life Care Homes, before the Special Committee on Aging, May 25, 1983.

Chapter 6

What To Do If A Nursing Home Is Necessary*

W hen and if the need for a nursing home does arise, it is crucial for you to know the type of information you will need, where to find it, and how to put it together to arrive at a sound, informed decision. This chapter is designed to help you do exactly that.

Selecting a nursing home for yourself, a spouse, parent, or friend is not the sort of thing anyone looks forward to. We hope you will have read the entire book before turning to this chapter, in order to investigate all possible alternatives.

*This chapter is condensed from *How to Evaluate and Select a Nursing Home*, by R. Barker Bausell and Michael Rooney, published by People's Medical Society. Copyright © 1983 by People's Medical Society. Reprinted with permission. For more information, see "Key Resources" at the end of this chapter.

One alternative we have not discussed until now is adult foster care. Adult foster care permits a person who is 60 years of age or older to be placed in a home setting with another individual or family. This individual or family would then provide all the care required. This can be an extremely useful program for the person who does not require intensive nursing services, provided a good placement is found. Such programs are normally operated and funded by local governments. For information about adult foster homes in your area contact your local Area Office or Department of Aging.

What Are Nursing Homes?

To begin with, the term nursing home is actually a very general name for several different types of medical-care facilities. It has the connotation of a "last stop" for the elderly, but it can actually be a place for people of all ages to convalesce following an accident or serious illness.

A nursing home is not for someone who is extremely sick—a hospital is. It is also not a prison, where people are segregated from society. It is not a drawn-out hospice program, where people are waiting for inevitable deterioration and death. It is rather a home for people who have difficulty caring for themselves, where rehabilitation on all levels is undertaken. As such, nursing homes provide three basic types of services:

- **nursing/medical care**—examples of which are injections of medication, catheterizations, and physical therapy, as well as other forms of rehabilitative services.

- **personal care**—for example, assistance in eating, dressing, bathing, getting in and out of bed, and even making telephone calls.

- **residential services**—such as providing a clean room, good food, and a pleasant atmosphere with appropriate social activities.

Nursing homes may be classified in many different ways. Generally speaking, the most common classifications are: 1) level of care they provide; 2) type of ownership; 3) the types of licensure/accreditation they possess.

Levels of Care

Different kinds of care are provided by nursing homes. Many facilities provide for both skilled and intermediate care, while some provide for additional custodial care on the same campus. Other homes specialize in providing a specific type of care.

Skilled-Nursing Facilities

In these facilities, care is delivered by registered and licensed practical nurses on the orders of an attending physician. Typical nursing and rehabilitation services include all of those listed in the Health Services Checklist which you will find in Appendix A. The person who requires skilled nursing is often bedridden and not able to help him/herself. An individual may be placed in a skilled-nursing facility for either a short or extended period of time, depending upon the prognosis.

Intermediate-Care Facility

The intermediate care facility provides less intensive care than skilled facilities. The cost is usually less than skilled nursing. The patient has a greater degree of mobility and normally is not confined to a bed. Care is also delivered by registered and licensed practical nurses (as well as an array of therapists). Intermediate care facilities stress rehabilitation therapy that will enable the patient to either return to a normal home setting or at least to regain and/or retain as many functions of daily living as possible. For these patients with chronic conditions, incapable of independent living, these facilities offer a full range of medical, social, recreational, and support services.

Ownership

There are basically three types of nursing-home ownership. Opinions differ with respect to which type offers the best quality of care, so we do not suggest that you choose or rule out a home based on this characteristic. It is just something you may want to consider.

Non-Profit. Non-profit homes are operated by various religious, fraternal, charitable, or community groups in accordance with the non-profit corporation statutes of the particular states in which they are located.

For-Profit. These homes are operated specifically in order to earn a profit for their investors (which may be an individual or a corporation). They may also be called proprietary nursing homes. These homes are definitely on the increase, accounting for a decided majority of currently operating homes.

Governmental/public non-profit. In some areas local or state governments operate nursing homes offering various levels of care. These homes are classified as public non-profit institutions, since they are funded through the collection of taxes or the sale of municipal bonds.

Licensure and Certification

The final way in which nursing homes differ from one another is in the type of licenses and/or certification they possess.

Basically, a nursing home license means that a facility has met certain standards established by law. It also means that the operators of the home agree to provide certain standards of care. Still another term you may run into is "accreditation," which again is very similar in meaning to the other two. Just because a home is licensed, certified, or accredited, does not mean that it provides high quality care. It only means that it met certain *minimal* standards on one particular day. Thus, while it is better to be officially licensed, certified, and accredited than not to be so, such stamps of approval don't always mean a great deal. What we are going to teach you to do in this chapter, therefore, is to rely on a form of accreditation that you *can* trust: your own!

Determining Health And Financial Status

Although this chapter is designed to help you choose a nursing home, there is one very important decision that must precede this task. You must decide if indeed a nursing home is the best option for the per-

son in question. Of almost equal importance is the need to determine
what you can afford. Selecting those services which you cannot
afford is simply a waste of time. Therefore, this chapter will help you
with the following:

- Show you how to systematically assess your, or your relative's
  physical needs, using the Health Status and Health Services
  checklists.

- Determine what you can afford by examining financial
  resources, income, and assets.

Assessing Health Care Needs

People often feel they have no real options when it comes to long-
term-care decisions. They may have been told that a nursing home is
absolutely essential by a physician or a hospital social worker and
consequently feel that the decision is a foregone conclusion.

Certainly, experienced, professional advice is important in a decision such as this, but there are often many extenuating circumstances. What may be true in general (or "on the average") may not
be true for you. You, the person in question, and perhaps other family members must decide for yourselves.

**First assess physical needs and then attempt to match available
resources within the home and the community to those needs.** This,
coupled with one's financial status can go a long way toward helping
you decide if nursing home care is the proper option.

To arrive at a thorough assessment of a person's condition there
are two general areas to consider: a person's general health status and
the type of health services needed. For your convenience we have
included several checklists in Appendix A to enable you to systematically determine an individual's health care needs. We do not expect
you to be an expert in every area. What we are suggesting is that you
consider each statement in terms of how it applies to you or your
relative, and then answer it to the best of your ability. You may want
to obtain professional help (such as your family physician or gerontological nurse) in completing the health status/services checklists.

Health status checklist
The "Health Status Checklist" in Appendix A covers activities of daily living, such as eating, bathing, walking, etc. As you read each statement on the checklist, consider how well the person in question (whether yourself or a relative) is able to perform each function. Then simply check those functions where the person experiences a problem. If unsure, indicate that statement with a question mark to remind yourself that you might want to seek professional advice. This will prove to be invaluable when you speak with institutional and noninstitutional providers. You will be able to describe the person's condition and needs in very precise terms, and make your screening process much easier.

Health services checklist.
Your next task is to complete the "Health Services Checklist" in Appendix A by answering "yes" or "no" to a series of statements concerning services the person may require. Once again you may seek professional help to complete this form; however, if you consider each statement in terms of what the person requires, then you should do just fine. Go back and count the number of "yes" answers you have under the different types of care. Generally speaking, the more "yes" answers in the intensive nursing care section, the more the person could be a candidate for institutional care. The important thing to remember is that you now have a basis for discussing the person's condition with home-based service agencies, as well as institutional-based providers.

Assessing Financial Status

Nursing home care is expensive. There is no question about it. Some homes are more expensive than others, so you must assess what you, the person to be placed, and his/her family are willing and able to pay. Then you must know how to screen facilities with this in mind and, finally, how to choose the best available home.

Some nursing homes are relative bargains, providing excellent care at a lower cost than the competition. Some are grossly overpriced and provide substandard care in return. Generally speaking, however, nursing home care is like everything else: The more you pay, the more you get. Thus, unless circumstances are truly dire, you should not pick a nursing home based solely on financial considerations.

Estimated Monthly Income Chart.
How much you can afford to pay may put limits upon your ultimate choice, so your task is to systematically assess the financial resources available to help support placement. Use the chart in Chapter 1 to work out the estimated monthly income. To help you fill it out, we have included here a detailed discussion of each item on the chart:

(1) **Social Security.** If the person in question (yourself or a relative) collects social security (or is eligible to collect it as a result of the crisis that precipitated the need for nursing home care), find out exactly how much his/her monthly checks amount to. Enter this figure into the chart.

(2) **Other Retirement Plans.** Do the same thing for the person's company or other retirement plan. If he or she is not receiving this (but is eligible), find out how to begin to tap this resource. (If you are not satisfied with an answer you receive over the phone, request that the company send you a detailed financial statement of the person's account plus his/her retirement contract). Enter this result on Line (2).

(3) **Private Insurance.** Some insurance plans cover care in a nursing home under certain circumstances (and for varying lengths of time). Read the policy carefully. In the event that coverage is available, make sure that he or she qualifies. If you are not satisfied with the answer received from the insurance company, contact your State Insurance Commissioner's Office or consult an attorney.

(4) **Bank Accounts, Stocks, Bonds, and other Liquid Assets.** You will need a thorough inventory of all the person's assets. If he or she is able to assist you, sit down and conduct a thorough interview, including where papers and other sources of information are stored. You must be thorough and persistent. If the person cannot supply all the information you need (or if some of it is suspect), then you must conduct an exhaustive search for all relevant documents.

Next, estimate the monthly income derived from these sources and enter those results on Line (4). (In other words, calculate what the monthly interest will be on the bank accounts, what the aveage monthly dividends are on stocks, and so forth. Be conservative, however, for most of these values fluctuate and it is better to underestimate your monthly income than overestimate it).

(5) **Old Debts Owed to the Person.** This is not a particularly reliable source of revenue, simply because old debts of any sort are hard to collect. If they are owed by relatives or friends, however, nostalgia or a sense of guilt may enable you to collect them in this time of need. (It is not wise to count this money until it is in hand.)

(6) **Real Estate.** In most cases, this means the house that the person is living in. There are several ways to derive some income from such an asset. The first is obviously to sell it and use either the principal or its interest. This may be a very traumatic step for the person, so approach this option carefully. (Try to avoid it altogether if there is a chance that the person someday might be able to live there again.)

The second possibility is to rent the property (if the individual is likely to be institutionalized long enough to make this worthwhile). A third possibility is to convert the home's equity into capital—as in the home equity conversion plans discussed in Chapter Two. In any case, a reputable real estate agent should be able to give you a reasonable estimate of either how much the property is worth or how much it is likely to sell for. Deduct 10-15% from these estimates to be safe and enter the results in the charts.

(7) **Antiques and Other Valuables.** You must definitely approach this area with caution. Do not even consider those objects with special sentimental value to the owner. It is also wise to consult with other family members especially those who might expect to inherit one of the items in question.

Antiques and valuables by themselves generate no income until they are sold. However, if family members agree, you may arrange to sell selected items over a given period of time. In this way you would realize a monthly income. If you sell all the items at once, then the money realized could be placed into an interest producing account and listed under item (4). In any event an antique dealer should be consulted to obtain an appraisal of the items.

(8) **Pledges from Other Family Members.** If the person in question has several children or other very close relatives, you should find out how much they are willing to contribute. Personal and family characteristics dictate how reliable these pledges will be, thus you may want to opt for a single payment to have something on hand. Generally speaking, however, most of us are better able to pay monthly installments.

(9) **Medicare.** Medicare is a federal health insurance program for persons over 65 that covers hospitals, skilled nursing care, physician services, home health care, and outpatient care. The program is administered by Social Security through the Health Care Financing Administration. Medicare will pay for skilled nursing care *only* if the following conditions are met:

- It must be a skilled nursing facility (SNF), and it must be certified to participate in the Medicare program.

- The person must have been in the hospital for at least three (3) days, and be admitted to the SNF within 30 days.

- A physician must certify that the person requires skilled care on a daily basis for the same or related reason they were hospitalized.

- There must be ongoing utilization review to determine if the person is receiving skilled nursing care.

- If a determination is made that skilled care is no longer required, Medicare coverage ceases.

You should also be aware that Medicare *is not* a long-term solution to paying for nursing-home care, since it does not cover intermediate or sheltered care. Medicare coverage for skilled care as of 1985 is as follows:

Time Frame in Days	Medicare Pays	You Pay*
1-20	100% of costs	Nothing
21-100	All but $50/day	$50/day
101 +	Nothing	All costs

*Amount of copayment is subject to change when social security law is amended.

If Medicare recipients exhaust their benefits for nursing-home care, they might want to consider applying for Medicaid coverage.

(10) **Medicaid.** Medicaid is an assistance program that is administered by the individual states through local welfare departments. The funds are part federal and part state and are intended primarily for low-income individuals requiring health-care services. Medicaid covers a wide range of health services, including both skilled and intermediate nursing-home care, provided the person is admitted to a nursing-home that is Medicaid certified.

Because Medicaid is state administered you will need to check the exact eligibility requirements of your state. Benefits are usually based upon the following: income, savings, property, and other assets. Once a nursing home accepts a Medicaid patient, it agrees to the Medicaid payment and will not attempt to collect the difference from the patient or the family. Medicaid rates are usually below going rates, and are established by the state. These rates are then agreed to by the nursing homes that participate in the program. Reimbursement will vary from state to state, and may vary within a state, so check your local situation closely.

Applications for a determination of Medicaid eligibility are submitted to the local welfare or public assistance office. The office will then determine the applicant's eligibility and notify you accordingly. In some cases, the local offices will assist you in finding a facility that accepts Medicaid patients. It is not at all unusual for *Medicare* patients to apply for *Medicaid* coverage once their skilled-nursing benefits have been exhausted.

(11) **Supplementary Security Income (SSI).** This is a public assistance program that applies to certain people who are legally blind, disqualified for work due to physical or mental disability for a twelve-month period, or who have severely limited financial resources. Requirements for this assistance can be relatively complicated to understand, so the best course of action is to contact your local social security or welfare office.

(12) **Union, Fraternal, or Veteran Benefits.** There are a number of miscellaneous sources for help, so the best advice we can give you is to leave no stone unturned. Search for documentation of eligibility for these sources and call the relevant organization. If you do not know whether a given organization offers such benefits, call

and find out. Often such conversations result in additional leads. (Some organizations, such as the Odd Fellows, the Masons, and church groups run their own system of nursing homes, which occasionally are less expensive than proprietary institutions.)

(13) **Gross Monthly Income.** In filling out the Estimated Monthly Income Chart, record your answers in the appropriate lines (1) to (12) and columns for present income, as well as expected income six months and two years from now. It is very important that you estimate future income, and we suggest the six-month and two-year intervals. Your answer should now be recorded in line (13), Gross Monthly Income. The next step is to make adjustments to the gross monthly income, which you will do in line (14), Obligations/ Expenses.

(14) **Obligations/Expenses.** Naturally you must also take into consideration any debts or ongoing expenses (such as insurance premiums) the person may have. Also, don't forget to include some routine spending money. Enter total expenses on line (14), and subtract this amount from line (13). Your answer on line (15) is the estimated Net Monthly Income, or the amount that is left over after all expenses are paid.

(15) **Net Monthly Income.** We have suggested that you estimate the person's present and future monthly income for several reasons. In the first place more, or fewer, sources of revenue may be available in the future. Second, certain sources such as Medicare and various types of insurance are good only for a certain fixed period of time (thus you will need to consider what will be available when those resources end).

Obviously, the more net income, the more you will have available to spend on service and the longer you can provide those services. Knowing the person's net income will be very important when you screen nursing homes to determine the total monthly charges. And finally, nursing home charges are subject to change and these charges are usually upward.

Total Assets and Net Worth Chart.
What is net worth? Simply put, net worth is the dollar value of a person's assets, minus any obligations, debts, or loss of value. You may be familiar with the terms "gross income" and "net income" from doing your federal, state, or local income taxes. Knowing the

dollar value of the person's assets can be very important, especially if you are seeking additional sources of income-generating assets.

By examining the person's total assets you can determine which ones are already in a form that could generate income, or be used to make a down payment on services. The most readily available, and spendable, asset is, obviously, cash. However, you must determine which other real assets could be converted into cash to help produce needed monthly income. Remember that antiques and jewels, while valuable, produce no income until they are sold, and the resulting funds invested in interest-bearing accounts. Therefore, you will want to examine carefully all the person's assets.

To help make your job easier, we suggest that you use the Total Assets and Net Worth Chart supplied in Chapter One. You will find the chart arranged in such a way that each asset can be listed on a separate line. A quick examination of the chart will reveal that it is nothing more than an inventory, although a very important inventory.

This chart is easier to use than the Estimated Monthly Income Chart that you have already completed. On lines (1) through (7) simply list the value of the assets that are shown; lines (8)(a) to (d) are for assets that do not fit the other categories. When you complete this section, put your answer on line (9).

While the Assets can be thought of as the *plus* side, we must also tell you that there is a *minus* side as well. You, or your older relative, no doubt, has incurred the normal living expenses, and these must be figured into your calculations. Here you want to list these items on lines (10)(a) to (d). Be sure to include such items as: unpaid balance on a mortgage, amount owed on an auto loan, unpaid taxes, etc.

When you have listed all these items then add lines (10)(a) to (d) and enter the total on line (11) in the space provided. The final step is to subtract line (11) Total Obligations/Debts/Loss of Value, from line (9), Gross Value of Assets. The resulting answer on line (12) will be the person's *total net worth*.

From the results of these two charts, you should be able to arrive at a reasonable estimate of the resources available and what can be afforded. These estimates must be tailored to the individual terms of the nursing homes you are considering. Some may require larger down payments than others, with relatively lower monthly fees. Others may be just the opposite. Once you deduct the amount of the down payment from the assets, then you can determine how much monthly income the remaining assets will produce. (Remember you must also deduct any debts owed). Make sure, however, that when you earmark an asset to apply toward a down payment, you deduct the income it would have generated from the Estimated Monthly Income Chart.

As you can see, all this can become quite complicated. If you do not have an aptitude for such planning, you may find it helpful to consult an accountant or financial planner. If you do not know where to find such a person, consult Appendix D for the address and telephone number of your Area Office on Aging. Many of these agencies can provide direct assistance or give you the names of agencies that can help.

Screening The Nursing Homes In Your Area

Let us assume that after considering all the alternatives, you have decided that a nursing home is necessary. Let us also assume that you are aware of the level of care that will be needed. It is now time to begin the process of choosing the best home to fit your particular needs.

Initial Screening

By now you have completed the health and financial checklists. As a result you have a good idea of the types of services required and your budget limitations. The next step is to match those needs to the services available in your area, while staying within your budget.

It is possible you have already resigned yourself to the fact that you or members of your family are going to have to visit several homes personally. Since this will be a very time-consuming task, and even unpleasant, it is essential that you do as much initial screening over the phone as possible.

For your convenience we have provided a Screening Chart (see Appendix B) to help you record the resulting information. This chart is designed to be very thorough. If you find it to be too detailed or too time-consuming for your purposes, then by all means use only those sections (or columns) that you find helpful.

In order to screen the nursing homes in your area we suggest the following strategy:

Decide realistically where the home can be located. You, or your older relative or spouse will need, and is entitled to, frequent visits from family members and friends. Try for convenience initially because constant contact with family is one of the most important considerations in long term care.

Obtain a list of all licensed facilities in your chosen region. This can be done by consulting the Yellow Pages of the phone directory or by contacting various agencies such as your State Office on Aging (see Appendix D), your local social security office, or the State Welfare Office. In addition, national directories such as *The U.S. Guide to Nursing Homes* are available at public libraries. Now refer to the Screening Chart in Appendix B and make plenty of copies.

On your copies of the Screening Chart in Appendix B, enter the names, addresses, and phone numbers of the results of the facilities found.

Make a list of those special nursing/personal services that the person is likely to need. Enter these in the blank slots under the Additional Monthly Services and Charges column on the second page of the Screening Chart, columns (1) to (9).

If not already available from the sources used to obtain the list of eligible homes (2), call each of the promising facilities to obtain the following information. Enter into corresponding columns on the Screening Chart:

Column (a): What level of care is offered (skilled or intermediate)? Obviously, if you need skilled nursing care and the home you have called does not provide it, you may terminate the call at this point. Circle the appropriate entries in column (a) of the Screening Chart.

Column (b): Are there special restrictions on the types of patients accepted? Even some skilled nursing homes are reluctant to accept patients who require a great deal of supervision so it is helpful to ascertain what restrictions, if any, are in operation. If not, simply write 'none' in column (b), or if there is some uncertainty, place a question mark in column (b).

Column (c): How many beds (of the type you need) does the home provide? Larger facilities generally offer a wider range of services. (Enter the appropriate figures for each level of care in which you are interested, or may be interested in the future, in column (c).

Column (d): Is there a waiting list, and if so, approximately how long is it? You may not have the luxury of being able to wait for an extensive period of time. However, if you are flexible in this regard, it is sometimes true that the best homes are the one with the longest waiting lists. Enter the answer in column (d).

Column (e): What type of license or accreditation/certification does the home have? Generally speaking, if the facility is not licensed by the state and certified for Medicare/Medicaid, do not consider it. The Joint Commission on the Accreditation of Hospitals (JCAH) conducts an exacting evaluation, so if the home is JCAH-accredited this may be a plus. (Make sure that none of the licenses/certifications are provisional in nature. This means that the home does not yet fully meet the minimum standards of the agency in question.) Circle either "yes" or "no," or Medicare/Medicaid under columns (e)(1) through (e)(3).

Column (f): Does the home accept Medicare and Medicaid? If the person qualifies for one of these programs you will want to know if the institution will accept them as full payment. Some homes, for example, have a restricted number of Medicare/Medicaid beds, so this can prove to be a stumbling block if they are filled. Enter the answer in columns (f)(1) and (f)(2).

Column (g): Is there an initial deposit/down payment required and if so, what is it? Some homes require a sizable down payment, others do not. If a particular home doesn't require this, just leave column (g) blank or enter zero. Otherwise, enter the dollar figure.

Column (h): What are the monthly room charges? These will probably differ with respect to whether you want a private or nonprivate room. It might be wise to enter both figures in columns (h)(1) and (h)(2).

Column (i): Are additional monthly services provided? What are their charges? You have already determined the special nursing/personal care needs required by the person. Write each of these in the space provided in columns (i)(1) though (i)(9). Determine if these entail special charges, and, if so, what are they per month? Enter the relevant figures in the appropriate columns.

Add the appropriate dollar figure from either column (h)(1) or (h)(2) (according to the type of room you desire) to those through (i)1 through (i)(9) and place the total in the final column. This will give you an estimate (probably an underestimate) of the total monthly cost of placing someone in this particular nursing home. This result, combined with the figure in column (g), should give you a rough idea as to whether or not you can afford the care in this home, when compared to the entries in your Estimated Monthly Income and Total Assets and Net Worth Charts.

Let us assume that you have narrowed the nursing homes in your area down to a manageable number by screening out those that are:

- too far away to allow you and other family members to visit the patient frequently;

- not properly certified/licensed;

- too expensive for your resources; and

- not appropriate in other ways, such as not offering the range of medical services the person needs.

Now comes the hard part! As we discussed in the previous chapter, there is absolutely no substitute for your own close, first-hand inspection. What you must now do, then, is to call those homes still under consideration for appointments. Make it clear that you not only want to talk to the homes' administrator but that you also plan to make an extensive tour of *all* the home's facilities. This will undoubtedly take several hours, so plan accordingly.

Preparing for the Visit

In the next few pages, you will find a long list of questions that can be answered by a simple "yes" or "no." These questions are divided into six general categories:

- the condition and layout of the building and the grounds;
- the qualifications and general demeanor of the personnel;
- the quality and atmosphere of the residents' rooms,
- the quality of the medical/nursing care offered;
- the recreational/social services available; and
- the quality of the food served.

Each of these categories contains a great many questions. You probably won't be able to answer them all after a single visit. You may not even want to, since some questions are more important than others (and some may seem completely irrelevant to some people).

What you should do, however, is to at least read and consider each of these questions well before your scheduled visit. If nothing else, they should provide some very good hints concerning important things to look for that you might not otherwise think of. They are taken from the writings of a number of experts including reports of common abuses found in actual visits by professional inspectors. Remember, the questions you are about to read do not need to be answered "yes" or "no"—they are for informational purposes.

They are arranged in a format that you can actually take with you to the nursing home you decide to visit. (You may prefer to duplicate this checklist rather than taking the entire book with you.) Don't feel hesitant about walking around, checklist in hand, while visiting a nursing home. If anyone objects or tries to embarrass you about this, that is a warning sign about how the facility is run.

You will note that the same checklist can be used for four different homes. We recommend that you do this, since having all the answers side by side should help you decide which home best suits your needs.

When you examine the checklist closely, you will note that some of the questions are starred. These questions can be answered only by your observations.

Remember that you don't necessarily have to answer every single question on the checklist. You should try very hard to answer the ones that are important to you. If you forget to ask something important during your visit, you can always call later and try to get the answer. If you find that you didn't observe something important, however, the only way to get the answer is to schedule another visit. The best thing to do is to look over the checklist carefully before you end each interview, to make sure you have asked and answered all the relevant starred questions. Then, look over the rest of the questions before you end your tour, to make sure that you have seen everything you need to see to answer the rest. We suggest that you don't rely on memory. Circle the answer to each question as you observe/ask it.

Buildings and Grounds
In many ways the physical layout of the building and grounds should be among the least important considerations in choosing a nursing home. The newest, brightest building with the most modern construction will soon fade into the background if what goes on inside does not promote the health and happiness of its residents.

Still, the building and the grounds can serve as an important negative indicator, if nothing else. A rundown, poorly maintained physical plant says a great deal about the administration's (or the ownership's) concern for its residents and perhaps something even more about the institution's financial solvency. Even with this in mind, however, beauty counts for far less than safety and livability.

Safety
Things to look for or ask about concerning the safety of the building and grounds are:

1. Does the building appear to be fireproof?

2. Are the sidewalks clean and walks maintained?

3. Are the emergency exits well marked?

4. Are there sufficient smoke detectors?

5. Is firefighting equipment (such as fire extinguishers and a sprinkler system) prominent?

6. Is there an actively functioning safety committee?

Livability

Whether or not a building is livable depends upon a number of different things, such as convenience, appearance, and the quality of life. Some things to look for in this area are:

1. Is the outside of the building neat and well maintained?

2. Do the sidewalks have wheelchair ramps?

3. Is the home located within easy walking of public transportation?

4. Does the neighborhood in which the home is located appear to be safe? (If in doubt, consult the local police).

5. Are the grounds spacious?

6. Are they well maintained?

7. Is there an area where residents can sit outside?

8. Do residents sit or walk outside (weather permitting)?

9. Does the entrance have handrails and wheelchair ramps?

10. Is the lobby clean and well furnished?

11. Do residents use the lobby?

12. Are the corridors clean and well maintained?

13. Are the corridors wide enough for two wheelchairs to pass easily?

14. Does there seem to be enough room in general for the residents?

The Rooms

Here we are getting into a much more crucial area. Many elderly residents are leaving their homes in which they have lived many years, substituting for them a single room (which they may have to share with one or more other residents). In a nursing home, a resident's room must become his/her castle. It is, therefore, very important what that room looks like and how homelike it can be made.

There are basically three things to look for when observing the rooms: the *comfort* they provide, the *atmosphere* they permit, and their *safety*. It is difficult to say that one of these aspects is more important than another, thus you should attend to all three.

Comfort

Although this category overlaps with what we call atmosphere, some things to find out are:

1. Are the rooms neat and clean?

2. Is there sufficient light?

3. Is there sufficient closet space?

4. Does each resident have a sink and mirror?

5. Is the room nicely furnished?

6. Is the room air conditioned?

7. Does the room have an individual thermostat?

8. Is there an adjoining bathroom?

9. Is this bathroom shared by no more than four other residents?

10. In general, do the residents have enough personal space?

11. If the rooms have TV sets, are they equipped with headsets?

Atmosphere

Few things are more important in the necessarily confining environment of a nursing home.

1. Do residents have a choice between single and jointly occupied rooms? (Undoubtedly a single room will be more expensive. It's not always preferable, however. Sometimes a compatible roommate provides very real companionship to a lonely, elderly resident.)

2. Are procedures for switching incompatible roommates liberal and clearly spelled out? (This question has two aspects.
   Every effort should be expended to begin with to insure
   compatibility—e.g. smokers should not be paired with non-
   smokers. Mistakes can happen, however, and there must be
   procedures to rectify those that cannot be worked out
   through counseling and compromise.)

3. Does each bed have a curtain or screen for privacy?

4. Do all the rooms have windows to the outside?

5. Are there curtains on the windows?

6. Is there counter space for personal objects?

7. Do the rooms have private telephones?

8. Do the bathrooms and toilet areas have adequate privacy?

9. Do residents hang their own pictures?

10. Do the beds have bedspreads?

Safety
In the rooms, as throughout the home, you should always be con-
scious of safety factors. For example:

1. Do all the rooms open to a hallway? (This is important both
   in case of fire and in insuring that the residents get prompt
   nursing care and are monitored as often as possible.)

2. Are there grab bars on the toilet and bath tub?

3. Do the tubs have nonslip surfaces?

The Personnel
No matter how impressive the physical layout of the building, no
matter how beautiful the grounds or how cheerful and spacious the
rooms, no nursing home can be a decent place to live or deliver high-
quality care if its staff is not qualified, dedicated, and well supervised.

Unfortunately, these things are far more difficult to judge than
anything we've discussed so far. People are far more complex than

buildings or rooms, so you will have to be very observant throughout your visit to be able to get a handle on the quality of the home's staff.

There are basically three things you can look for: the availability of key personnel, their qualifications, and their demeanor toward the residents. All three of these factors are important, and all three are reflected in the questions that follow.

The answers to most of the following questions should be 'yes,' since in many cases they are mandated by law, but it still doesn't hurt to ask. As we pointed out earlier, just because something is required for certification doesn't necessarily mean that it will actually be present in an officially certified/licensed home. Here are some specific questions to ask.

1. Does the home's administrator have a current license?

2. Does the home employ:

   a. a physical therapist?

   b. an occupational therapist?

   c. a speech pathologist?

   d. a dietitian?

   e. a nurse practitioner?

3. Is the nursing supervisor a Registered Nurse? (This is generally mandated by law and is a good idea.)

4. Are all the heads R.N.s? (The more registered nurses on staff, the better. In many homes, direct patient care is generally given by other personnel, but a large R.N. contingent is definitely a good sign.)

5. Do there seem to be enough nurses, nurses' aides, and orderlies on duty? (Many nursing homes find it difficult to attract and retain good nursing personnel. The home that is chronically shorthanded cannot deliver very good care.)

A few more things to consider are:

6. Was the administrator or his/her representative courteous to you?

7. Did he/she see you promptly?

8. Were the home's administrative policies well explained? (A written list is quite helpful.)

9. Was the administrator open to your questions?

10. Was the staff generally friendly toward you?

11. Was the staff neatly dressed?

12. Did the residents seem at ease with the staff?

13. Did the staff speak to the residents in respectful, noncondescending terms?

14. Did the staff seem to like the residents?

15. Did the staff generally look pleasant and cheerful?

Medical/Nursing Care
If you need to place a person in a skilled-nursing facility, chances are the quality of the medical/nursing care offered you by the home is by far its most important characteristic to you. The quality of care available to a home's residents is very closely related to the quality of the available staff.

We have chosen to divide our medical and nursing care questions into three general categories: the types of care available (which includes the personnel who deliver it); patient rights as they relate to medical care (which includes the right to seek alternative forms of care); and the physical or nontechnical care which the residents appear to receive.

Availability. You will have to ask either the home's administrator or the nursing director most of these questions, since they are not readily observable.

1. Is a physician on the premises for a fixed time each day? (Generally, it is better to have a physician on the premises rather than on call.)

2. Is a physician on call 24 hours a day? (This is an absolute. Generally it is more realistic if this duty is shared by a team of physicians, since it is very difficult for a single person always to be on call.)

3. Are there facilities outside of the residents' rooms for physical examinations?

4. Is a registered nurse on duty during the day, seven days a week?

5. Is at least one R.N. and one L.P.N. on duty day and night?

6. Are dental services provided in the home itself? (The dental health of elderly people is often a woefully neglected area. Studies have shown that very few older Americans receive proper dental care, whether they are in nursing homes or not. You shouldn't assume that old age means that tooth loss is inevitable. Many experts say that if you have most of your teeth by age 50, there is no reason why you shouldn't keep them for the rest of your life.)

7. Does the home have access to one pharmacist who maintains records on each resident and reviews them when new medications are ordered? (This is a very important concern, due to the real possibility of drug toxicity among the elderly. If the drugs a resident takes are not carefully monitored, with someone being responsible for his monitoring, serious difficulties can occur.)

8. Is a separate room set aside for storing and preparing drugs?

9. Does the home have a contract with an ambulance service?

10. Does the home keep its own medical records?

11. Is there a formal health education program for residents? Nursing homes are almost inevitably set up to encourage passivity and dependence in their residents, even with the best of possible motives. Residents should be encouraged to take as much responsibility for their own care and health as possible, so formal programs designed for this purpose are very important.

12. Does the home provide for frequent continuing education programs for its staff? (New advances are constantly being made in long-term care, so it is very important that these new findings are shared with the staff. This also helps to promote professionalism among the health care givers.)

Patient Rights. Great strides have been made in this area in recent years. The federal government requires that all nursing homes subscribe to a formal Patient's Bill of Rights, in order to qualify for Medicare/Medicaid payments. Your job will not be so much to see what the home officially subscribes to (a patient's bill of rights, after all, is only a sheet of paper), but to see how the home translates its philosophy to its actual dealings with patients.

Specific things to ask about these are:

1. Does the home subscribe to (and provide you with a copy of) a patient's bill of rights?

2. Does the resident (or resident's family) have free access to his/her medical records?

3. May the resident select his/her own physician? (It's important to find out if the resident's personal physician is willing to continue seeing him/her after being admitted to a nursing home. If you find that you must depend upon the home's medical staff for whatever reasons, make sure that you interview the physician who will be overseeing the person's care.)

4. May the resident select his/her own hospital? (There is more variability among hospitals than most people realize. Some are excellent and some are very bad. Make sure that your choice of a nursing home doesn't result in the choice of a substandard acute-care hospital.)

5. Does the home make arrangements for private duty nurses when the family thinks one is required?

6. Does the home have policies which severely restrict the use of physical restraints?

.7. Are the vast majority of the residents free of physical restraints? (There are occasions when a resident must be restrained for his/her own good. We believe that these occasions are rare, however, and that physical restraints should never be used to justify staffing shortages.)

8. Are arrangements made for patients who wish to use alternative professional services (such as podiatrists or chiropractors)?

9. Are you allowed to make alternative arrangements for purchasing prescription drugs? (You can often save a great deal of money if you purchase the person's drugs at a discount pharmacy rather than through the home's facilities.)

The Physical Nontechnical Care

Most of the nursing care received in any nursing home is quite routine in nature, such as bathing patients, changing soiled sheets, and so forth. Most of it is delivered by untrained (and sometimes inexperienced) nursing aides or orderlies. Never think for a minute, however, that the quality of this type of care isn't just as important as the most sophisticated medical procedures.

If anything, it is even more important as far as the resident's dignity, self-esteem, and comfort is concerned. Furthermore, poor physical care and hygiene can very easily lead to life-threatening situations, such as infections (a constant threat in nursing homes) and other types of illnesses. Be very vigilant, therefore, in answering the following questions:

1. Are the rooms and halls free of unpleasant odors? (Here, as always, you should be more concerned with the general state of affairs than single, isolated instances. In an institution serving ill, incontinent patients, an occasional unpleasant odor is inevitable. If you find this in several rooms or on several halls, however, you probably won't want the person subjected to such an environment.)

2. Do the rooms smell of heavy perfume? (One way to solve (1) above without providing a clean, comfortable environment is simply to spray heavy disinfectants everywhere. Another source of such smells might be heavy, unhealthy use of insecticides).

3. Does each resident's bed have a call button within easy reach? Can it be turned off only at the beside? Jean Nassau, whose *Choosing a Nursing Home* (Funk & Wagnalls, 1975) we definitely recommend, is adamant on this point. She believes that call buttons that can be turned off at the nursing station are just too easy to ignore by busy or apathetic staff.)

4. Are the bathrooms and bathing areas equipped with call buttons?

5. Does each resident have a water container and a clean glass in his/her room?

6. Are the more inactive residents' fingernails trimmed (and in the case of males, are their faces cleanly shaven)?

Recreational/Social Arrangements

Although you may not be as concerned about this area as the quality of the home's medical/nursing care, don't forget that you are in the process of choosing a nursing home. Certainly it is important that the person receive high-quality care, but it is also important that he/she be permitted to live in a pleasant, homelike atmosphere.

There is no question that the words nursing home conjure up mainly unpleasant thoughts and impressions. A nursing home can have certain advantages over other types of living arrangements, however, and these are chiefly social in nature. A well-run recreational/social program can add significantly to the quality of any elderly person's life.

Formal Programs
As is usually the case, some of these questions are best asked directly, some are best observed:

1. Does the home employ a full-time social director?

2. Are residents included in the planning of recreational/ social events in some formal way?

3. Is there an actively functioning patient council?

4. Does there seem to be a wide range of recreational/social activities planned?

5. Does there appear to be sufficient room for residents to engage in these activities?

6. Are calendars of these events posted in convenient places?

7. Are any events scheduled at night? (Remember, residents live at a nursing home 24 hours a day.)

8. Did you observe a substantial number of residents engaging in recreational/social events?

9. Are religious services held on the premises?

10. Are arrangements made to allow residents to attend outside religious services if they wish?

11. Are social services (such as counseling) available to both residents and their families?

12. Does the home sponsor frequent outings for residents who are able to go?

13. Does the home have any special programs with area schools or other organizations to bring young people into the home?

14. Is there a library with recent magazine issues and a good selection of books?

15. Is there a canteen?

Atmosphere
Again, these type of questions are difficult to answer, but are very important.

1. Do the published rules and regulations seem reasonable to you?

2. Are visiting hours for families and friends liberal?

3. Is there a quiet, private place where residents can entertain visitors?

4. Are residents permitted to entertain friends in their rooms?

5. Are members of the opposite sex permitted to visit one another in their rooms with the doors closed?

6. Is alcohol permitted in the home?

7. Are children permitted to visit?

8. Are residents permitted unlimited telephone calls (both incoming and outgoing)?

9. Are residents given reasonable leeway in establishing when they go to bed?

10. Do residents appear to socialize with one another?

11. Are there 'No smoking' areas designated in the home and are these regulations adhered to?

12. Is there a newsletter for families of residents?

The Food

Although it may seem like a minor consideration to you, an elderly person's meals are a crucial part of his/her life. This is especially true of an institutionalized person, perhaps because meals help break up the routine, perhaps because there are so few other sensory experiences which they can enjoy. Whatever the reasons, food is important to nursing home residents. Research has also shown that it is also their most frequently voiced complaint, so it will be worth your while to assess this aspect of the home's services. We suggest that you judge the food in two ways: the *sanitation* with which it is prepared and the *esthetic appeal/nutritional value* of the final product.

Sanitation
The importance of sanitation in the preparation of anyone's food is obvious. In institutional living, especially when the population is notoriously susceptible to gastrointestinal problems as well as infections, it is doubly important, so make sure you observe the following points:

1. Does the kitchen seem clean by your standards? (You should make a point of touring the kitchen, preferably during the preparation of a meal. Be on the lookout for unrefrigerated and improperly covered food.)

2. Does the kitchen have a dishwashing machine?

3. Are the kitchen staff neatly dressed?

4. Are the food carts closed for sanitation purposes?

5. Is the dining area clean?

Esthetic Appeal/Nutritional Value

Foods serves both physical and social functions for all people. Food that is poorly prepared or served in unappealing surroundings is not likely to be consumed, regardless of its nutritional content. To judge the home's nutritional standards, you should study its menu cycle, which should be both varied and not laden with cheap, starchy food.

1. Can the kitchen accommodate special (medically prescribed) diets?

2. Can it accommodate special, nonmedically (such as for religious or philosophical reasons) prescribed diets?

3. Does the kitchen ever prepare a resident's favorite dish as a treat?

4. Are residents served in their rooms if they prefer?

5. Is help available in both resident's rooms and in the dining area if they need help with eating?

6. Is the dining area attractive?

7. Are the tables convenient for wheelchair use?

8. Is there any flexibility as to when residents can eat?

9. Are dining hours reasonable (for example, breakfast should not be served at 6:00 a.m.)?

10. Are residents given sufficient time to eat their meals?

11. Does the food appear appetizing to you?

12. Do the residents seem to enjoy their meals?

13. Are snacks available between meals and at bedtime?

14. Do residents have access to a refrigerator to store their own snacks?

15. Is there a menu cycle available showing several weeks of meals?

16. Does this cycle seem to be sufficiently varied?

17. Does the meal being served match the one announced on the menu? (You want to make sure that the menu isn't just to impress visitors).

18. Are fresh fruits and vegetables served in season?

19. Does the home prepare meals from 'scratch' rather than employ frozen or prepackaged meals? (Would you want to eat frozen dinners the rest of your life? Would you always want to be served dehydrated mashed potatoes or eggs? It is also important that meals be served on real dishes, not throwaway plastic materials.)

20. Are residents given a choice of dishes?

These are some of the things you may want to find out about during your visit to those nursing homes you have decided are most likely to meet your needs. Don't expect to ask or remember every single question—the questions are to be used as a guide to visiting and as a memory jog when you are recollecting your visit.

The Contract

We have previously discussed the importance of determining exactly how much you or a family member can afford to pay for nursing care. We also discussed how to screen homes in your area to get a rough idea regarding how much they charge for their care.

Although helpful, this latter figure will probably be an underestimate of how much any given home will actually charge for the placement. Generally speaking, the basic charge you are given over the phone will cover those services required by all residents regardless of their particular needs. It is absolutely essential that you obtain a complete list of what does and does not entail extra charges as well as exactly what those charges are. There can be an advantage in selecting a home that has as few extra charges as possible. This applies when you consider that extra charges, like all others, are likely to increase over time.

Regardless of the name it goes by, any document which the nursing home administrator presents to you for your signature is a contract between you and that nursing home. Examine this contract carefully. If there are sections that you do not understand, have them explained (and possibly examined by an attorney). Make sure that all extras and promises are included in the contract or specified in a signed letter. (If you have an attorney, have this reviewed as well; if you cannot afford one but feel you need expert advice, contact your state or local department of aging or your local welfare office for assistance.)

Even if you feel you understand everything in the contract, we still suggest that you take it home and study it before signing. There should be no resistance to this: if there is, *beware.* Also be wary of contracts that clearly state your responsibilities and liabilities, but don't specify very much about what the home will provide nor what its responsibilities are. Make sure that you know what the penalties are if the person leaves early and make sure that if cash or other assets are entrusted to the home, details of how they will be used and accounted for are clearly specified (and of course that these details are agreeable to you). If there is some point in the contract that you do not like or makes you uncomfortable, ask to have it changed. You may not succeed, but it won't hurt to try.

Finally, at the risk of being repetitious, make sure that you have a clear understanding of the financial arrangements you are about to enter into *and* that you can live with those arrangements. To fail to do this will doom all your other efforts to failure.

After the Visit

If you have completed the above checklist it may appear as though you have found out everthing there is to know about the home you have just visited. There is more to choosing a nursing home, however, than just answering questions. Your overall impressions of the home and its different services are equally important, so we suggest that you do the following things as soon after your visit as possible.

Find a quiet place where you can work.

Review the questions and answers under each of the six categories in the checklist.

Attempt to rate each of the six categories according to the scale:

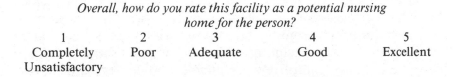

1	2	3	4	5
			Good	
Completely	Poor	Adequate	(Improvement	Excellent
unsatisfactory		(barely)	possible)	

Using these individual ratings, try to come up with an overall rating of the nursing home. Try to answer the following question:

Overall, how do you rate this facility as a potential nursing home for the person?

1	2	3	4	5
Completely	Poor	Adequate	Good	Excellent
Unsatisfactory				

There is no magical way to come up with this important rating. In the final analysis, you (with input from the potential resident if he/she is not yourself and is able to provide it), must decide how to weigh the importance of the different categories. A single "unsatisfactory," for example, on some categories might be enough to remove a home from serious consideration for most people. For others, the quality of the medical/nursing care provided (Category IV) or even the recreational/social services provided (Category V) may completely overshadow all others.

Further Considerations

If you still find it difficult to decide between the homes you visited, examine the reason for the problem. Is it because none are really suitable and you have to choose between the lesser of several evils? If so, consider visiting some more homes, possibly making a more systematic effort to get recommendations from acquaintances and health professionals.

Even if you have now made a final choice, there are still a number of important things you should do:

Discuss the situation with the person. If you are looking into nursing homes on behalf of another family member, we have suggested that you consider the person's preferences throughout the decision making process. It is now absolutely imperative that you discuss this important event with him/her, even if you are not one hundred percent sure that what you say will be fully understood. It is still important to try to explain the situation truthfully. White lies won't protect in the long run. If anything, they will simply increase anxiety and may even adversely affect the person's already tenuous orientation.

Understand the terms of your agreement with the nursing home. We have already stressed the importance of closely examining your contract, of determining exactly what the home's basic charges cover, and of ascertaining the price of those services that are not so covered. If you have any last-minute questions, discuss them with the home's administrator prior to signing the contract. To be safe, get all important points in writing, including what will happen if the person finds life in the home completely untenable and leaves earlier than planned.

Continue your role of inspector. Just because conditions seemed satisfactory on your announced visit does not mean that they will remain so. If you are visiting a relative in a home, in addition to careful observations during your normal visiting hours, occasionally plan to arrive unannounced to get a better view of exactly what goes on at the home when family is not normally present. Recheck some of the more important items on the checklist to make sure that conditions remain optimal.

Serve as the person's advocate. A very sick, or very old person who is almost totally dependent upon the home's staff for even the most basic services is not in a very good position to insist upon his or her rights or to judge whether or not appropriate care is being delivered. This must be a family member's job. If you observe a problem, call it to the appropriate person's attention immediately. (It is often easier to solve a small problem when it first arises than to wait and let it become a major bone of contention.) When possible, try to solve any problems within the home first. Seek the help of the Director of Nursing or the home's chief administrator if other approaches don't work. If this fails, family members should contact your nursing home ombudsman. Each state is mandated by law to have one. These professionals, whose addresses and phone numbers are listed in Appendix E, are specially trained to help work out any dispute you may have with your nursing home. (Most problems are solvable if you have the resolve to be firm and see them through to a satisfactory conclusion.)

Visit often. It is very important that you or your older relative not feel filed away and forgotten. Family members should visit as often as possible and encourage friends and relatives to do the same. Even patients who are disoriented or who do not seem to recognize family members respond to being touched and spoken to. Visits from those who care are often more important than all of modern medicine's technologies combined.

Key Resources

The chapter you have just read is condensed from a 107-page soft-cover edition of *How to Evaluate and Select a Nursing Home.* This detailed and extremely helpful book is available at cost for $4.95 from:

> People's Medical Society
> 14 East Minor Street
> Emmaus, PA 18049
> (513) 967-2136

The Society publishes this guide as part of a series of health action kits. The kits are for people to refer to when they need information about a particular problem or about the health-care system. If you are interested in finding out about other kits or publications, contact PMS.

There are very few directories or books on choosing a nursing home that are national in scope. You should ask a local librarian for a directory to homes in your area. The authors of this chapter recommend the following book, even though it is several years old:

Jean B. Nassau, *Choosing a Nursing Home*,
New York, Funk and Wagnalls, 1975.

References

Brotman, Herman B., *Every Ninth American*. Washington, D.C.:
Special Committee on Aging, United States Senate, February 1981.

Burger, Sarah Green, and Martha D'Erasmo, *Living in a Nursing Home*. New York: The Seabury Press, 1976.

Galton, Lawrence, *Don't Give Up on an Aging Parent*. New York:
Crown, 1975.

Grosset & Dunlap, *U.S. Guide to Nursing Homes*, 1970.

Harrington, Geri, and Ty Harrington, *Never Too Old*. New York:
Times Books, 1981.

Horn, Linda, and Elma Griesel, *Nursing Homes: A Citizen's Action Guide*. Boston: Beacon Press, 1977.

How to Select a Nursing Home, U.S. Health Care Financing Administration, Division of Long Term Care, Washington, D.C.: U.S. Government Printing Office.

Kleinfield, N. R., "New Approach to Health Care," *New York Times*, July 19, 1983.

_____ "The Home Health Care Boom," *New York Times*, July 21, 1983.

LaViolette, Suzanne, "Nursing Home Chains Scramble for More Private Paying Patients," *Modern Health Care*, May 1983: 130-138.

Moore, Thomas, "Way Out Front on Nursing Homes," *Fortune*, June 13, 1983: 142-150.

Nassau, Jean Barron, *Choosing a Nursing Home*. New York: Funk & Wagnalls, 1975.

Pennsylvania Department of Health, State Health Plan, 1981-1986. "Utilization Patterns & Financial Characteristics of Nursing Homes in the United States," National Health Survey, Series 13, No. 53, Hyattsville, Md.: National Center for Health Statistics, U.S. Department of Health & Human Services, August 1981.

Chapter 7

Choices And Chances

Coming Down to the Wire

If you've read through all or even some of the preceding chapters, you should know a good deal more about housing and living options than before. You may feel a bit uncertain about some of the details—exactly which features belong to which type of housing, etc. That's par for the course when you're taking in a great deal of new information at one time. Don't expect to remember everything, but you may want to reread some chapters—if not now, then later on, when some event in your life makes them newly relevant to you or your family.

Perhaps reading the guide helped you conclude that you—or your parents, or other older relatives—don't really need to make any major changes in your living arrangements for the time being. Or that the realities of what's available make staying put a decidedly more attractive option. Maybe you've discovered, too, that staying put is easier than moving, if you can use some of the benefits or services we've discussed. If little or no change is your choice at this time, you at least have a headstart on preparing for changes, when and if they do occur.

Perhaps you're convinced that some sort of change *is* in order, but are still unsure about which of the living arrangements presented here is most compatible with your needs. The best approach should be to contact some of the key resources listed at the end of each chapter. Get in touch with at least one organization related to each housing arrangement you have not definitely screened out. You may also want to get the recommendations of some of the groups that promote the interests of older citizens, listed in Appendix C at the back of the book.

To review them one more time, here are some of the outstanding factors that will probably guide your interests and your eventual decisions:

Your Age

Your age right now is a key factor. Most professional counselors agree that the best time to start planning for retirement is about age 45. Most people resist this advice.

To most 45 year-olds, old age is still a very long way off. Many 45 year-old parents are still concentrating on raising or launching their offspring into independent adulthood—paying for educational expenses, helping out with a first job, a first home, a wedding. Most are looking forward to a period of freedom, as parental responsibilities phase out and this is the time when many couples renew their relationship, perhaps activating some long-postponed plans that were set aside during the child-rearing years. It is difficult to begin scrimping and sacrificing for old age as soon as the last child exits the nest.

Although there is a reluctance to start planning early, it's wise to remember that *getting information costs nothing*! Some professionals who work with older families suggest that there are "critical" age points, when decisions about change come to a head. One such point is at about 70. At this age, health and financial limitations often catch up with people and impel them toward low-cost, convenient housing that provides increased services and security.

The major problem here is that waiting lists for many housing programs are *very* long—up to *ten years* in some large cities! This means that if you think you might possibly want to enter a low-cost housing program in your area at 70, you must begin to act at 60! Somewhat shorter waiting lists are the rule in other cities and in some of the retirement communities of the type discussed in Chapter Five. The small group residences described in Chapter Four usually entail less waiting. The same is true of home sharing, if you are the home seeker.

Your health
Your health and the health of other family members is another weathervane. If you have had no serious illness, are in top condition and have a family history of longevity, then the odds for living a long, healthy life are on your side.

The developers of one network of life-care homes point out that people who reach 75 without a major illness have excellent chances of living at least ten more years. And 75 is the age when a great many of these people arrive at the decision to enter some kind of communal living arrangement. Most people are eligible for these communities at 65 or earlier, if they've chosen early retirement. Thinking ahead when you are 60 or 65 turns out to be extremely important if you plan to make some changes some ten years down the line. People who live to be *very* old are likely to experience some amount of disability toward the end of their lives. If you make it to 90, (and more and more people will) you'll probably need a degree of assistance *before* then with maintaining your surroundings and, perhaps, yourself.

If you—or an older relative—are already living with one or more chronic health condition (even if they're under control), you *know* you must prepare for the future. You know that in time you'll probably want to have assistance with homemaking, indoor and outdoor maintenance, transportation, some type of in-home health care or a live-in housemate. You can start finding out right now whether your present living arrangements and your present community offer what you'll be needing in the future.

Your finances
While nothing is certain in life, your finances are probably more predictable than your health. That is why we stress filling out the Estimated Monthly Income and Total Assets and Net Worth charts in Chapter One, at the end of the book. Sometimes people postpone doing this because they are afraid the results will be negative. That isn't necessarily so—checklists can often show you assets you were not aware existed.

Facing your limitations is the hardest step in making realistic choices. You may have to rule out retiring to a retirement community in the sunbelt. However, you or other members of your family may come to focus on some innovative arrangement you hadn't thought of, such as house sharing, home equity conversion or a small group residence.

Your Social Needs
Social and emotional needs don't make such compelling arguments as health and finances, but they are no less important. Friendship and satisfying social contact are vital to enjoying life. Many people have deliberately chosen to remain near friends and family, even at financial sacrifice. Whether it is better to brave cold winters to be near your familiars or arrive as a stranger in a balmier clime, only you can decide. But don't subordinate your needs for active social contact to other considerations.

It's Your Decision, But (What Other People Say)

You alone, or—if you are married—you and your spouse have the first and last words on decisions relating to your lives. But, this doesn't mean that other parties should not be consulted or asked to help. Independence doesn't mean having to do it all alone. It does mean that you should mobilize your resources and use them to your own best advantage. When other people tell you what they think, you can certainly listen, weigh what they say and decide if and how to use whatever they contribute.

As you decide to change your living arrangements in some significant way, you should expect to encounter reaction from family and friends, whether you ask for them or not. Grown children who are genuinely concerned can take a responsible role by sharing in fact-gathering and helping sift through possibilities. It may be useful to bounce some of your ideas off your children and listen to their responses.

Remember, though, that your children and other family members will respond to your decisions in terms of their own needs and preferences. Their view of what's best for you is, understandably, colored by their own way of looking at the world and by their own stage of life. If family members disapprove of your plans, ask them to be very specific about just what it is they consider disagreeable. Don't get defensive. Just ask questions. Reassure them you'll carefully consider what they say. And you should consider carefully. Don't be intimidated by family disapproval when you (and your spouse) have reached your decision after careful study, thought, and discussion.

If you and an older family member are considering a decision about new living arrangements, do let that older person know how you feel and why. Even though such discussions can sometimes be difficult and quite disturbing, it is especially important to talk openly about what kinds of financial assistance or assistance with day-to-day living you wish to offer, and if that is a factor in the other person's plans. If an older person will be either increasing or decreasing the way and amount they depend on you because of this decision, both of you can only benefit by fully and thoroughly discussing what the move will mean to each.

Professionals you deal with—your lawyer, financial adviser or physician—will also offer opinions. Heed what they say and calculate that advice into your decision. The important thing about professionals is to depend only on those who represent *your* interests. As we have stressed, real estate developers and retirement home managers are not working for *you*, but for their companies. You should pay attention to what they say, but don't accept the agent as your personal adviser, no matter how understanding he/she seems. That is part of their job.

If you need an objective appraisal of the personal side of the situation, a retirement counselor, family counselor or member of the clergy may be a very good advisor. These individuals will have your interests at heart and can be sufficiently detached to stand back and take a perspective. They are in an excellent position to point out possible consequences of the move you're contemplating to you and your family.

Getting Ready for A Move

Suppose you've decided to relocate. Perhaps you're moving to another community or another part of the country, or maybe you've decided to sell your house and start afresh in a small apartment in your own community. Chances are your mood is optimistic because the move is of your own choosing—one you believe will improve the quality of the years ahead.

But don't be discouraged if you find yourself experiencing some signs of stress as you go about preparing to relocate. Even the best of moves is stressful. Every move involves separation and loss—of people, places, and objects to which you've become attached. Experiencing these feelings doesn't mean there is anything wrong with either you or the decision you've made. After a time most of these feelings will resolve themselves.

Whether or not you're anxious about entering a new community, there are some things you can do right now, *before* you move, that may help you feel more confident and less like a stranger in a new place. Think about the associations or activities that have given you the most pleasure and satisfaction in the past, and try to duplicate these as closely as you can, in your new location.

If you've belonged to social, religious, or athletic organizations of any kind, you will want to find out whether there are local chapters in your community. If not, you'll want to find out about groups that do similar kinds of things. Get in touch with a few groups a month or six weeks before you move, letting them know of your interest and your approximate date of arrival. Tell them you plan to contact them again shortly after you move to your new home.

In many cases, you will immediately receive a personal response that should make you feel much more at ease and at home in your new surroundings. If not, you've paved the way for a response when you arrive and do contact new groups. It helps, of course, if you already know someone in your new location or if you've already been given a personal reference from someone in your present community. Another way of accomplishing the same goal is to go to your public library and consult the Yellow Page section of the phone book for your new community. Look under Clubs, Associations, Churches and Synagogues, or the Information and Referral section of the phone book.

Even if you are busy packing, disposing of possessions and saying important goodbyes, the time you take to make these contacts before your move will be well worth it. Don't leave it all to the Welcome Wagon—you'll feel more in charge if you take the first few steps on your own.

Remember—the sound research and planning that went into your decision gives you a good headstart on adjusting to your new life and surroundings. Skilled planning may not guarantee the future, but it will make you more confident and resourceful in meeting whatever surprises the future holds.

Appendix A

Health Checklists

*Health Status Checklist**

Read each statement very carefully before deciding if it applies to the person in question, then place a check mark in front of those items that describe the person's condition. Does this person have difficulty with:

1. **Bathing**—requires assistance.

2. **Continence**—Difficulty in controlling either bladder or bowels.

3. **Dressing**—requires assistance or does not dress at all.

4. **Eating**—requires assistance, either from a person or via tube or intravenously.

5. **Mobility**—requires assistance to walk or confined to chair/ bed.

6. **Using toilet**—requires assistance or does not use at all.

*Suggested by the Department of Health and Human Services, Long Term Care Survey.

7. **Speech**—completely lost or so severely impaired that can be understood only with difficulty (cannot carry on a normal conversation).

8. **Hearing**—completely lost or so impaired that only a few words or loud noises can be heard.

9. **Vision**—blindness or so severely impaired that television set cannot be seen from 8 to 12 feet away (features of a familiar person recognized only within 2 to 3 feet).

10. **Mental status**—cannot understand (or remember) simple instructions, requires constant supervision or restraints for his/her own safety.

*Health Services Checklist**

This checklist requires that you consider the person's condition in terms of health services required. Each statement can be answered "yes" or "no". Once again, use your best judgment in determining your answers. This checklist will provide additional information that will be quite valuable when discussing the types of services available from the agencies and nursing homes you contact.

Intensive Nursing Care—Although all these services can be rendered at home, all require special training; most have a certain amount of risk associated with them, no matter who administers them.

Yes	No	Does the person require:
____	____	1. Bowel/retraining (needed when the patient is chronically incontinent).
____	____	2. Catheterization (needed when the patient cannot empty bowels/bladder unassisted)
____	____	3. Full bed bath (needed when the patient is entirely bed bound).
____	____	4. Intravenous injections (usually requires a tube connected to a vein for an extended period of time).
____	____	5. Oxygen therapy (for patients who cannot breathe with ease unassisted).
____	____	6. Tube or intravenous feeding (for patients who cannot eat even with assistance).

*Suggested by the Department of Health and Human Services, Long Term Care Survey.

Other Nursing Care—These services also require training, but generally not as much as intensive nursing care. They also do not nomally carry the same degree of risk.

Yes   No   Does the person require:

_____ _____ 1. Application of sterile dressing or bandages.

_____ _____ 2. Vital sign monitoring (blood pressure, temperature, pulse, respiration).

_____ _____ 3. Enema.

_____ _____ 4. Hypodermic injections

_____ _____ 5. Irrigation (wash wounds or body cavities).

Personal Care—These services require much less training and involve much less risk than the above two categories, but are often quite labor-intensive and time-consuming.

Yes   No   Does the person require:

_____ _____ 1. Administration of medications.

_____ _____ 2. Help with bathing, dressing, or eating.

_____ _____ 3. Rub or massage.

_____ _____ 4. Special diet.

Therapy Services—These services are performed by licensed, professionally trained therapists.

Yes   No   Does the person require:

_____ _____ 1. Physical therapy.

_____ _____ 2. Occupational therapy.

_____ _____ 3. Speech therapy.

_____ _____ 4. Psychological therapy

Appendix B

Nursing Home Screening Chart

SCREENING CHART

Nursing Home	(a) Level of care	(b) Restricted admissions	(c) Number of beds	(d) Waiting list	(e) Licensed (1) State	(e) Certified (2) Medicare Medicaid	(e) Accredited (3) JCAH	(f) (1) Accept Medicare	(f) (2) Accept Medicaid
	Skilled		——	—— Mos.	Y	Medicare	Y	Y	Y
	Inter-mediate		——	—— Mos.	N	Medicaid	N	N	N
	Skilled		——	—— Mos.	Y	Medicare	Y	Y	Y
	Inter-mediate		——	—— Mos.	N	Medicaid	N	N	N
	Skilled		——	—— Mos.	Y	Medicare	Y	Y	Y
	Inter-mediate		——	—— Mos.	N	Medicaid	N	N	N
	Skilled		——	—— Mos.	Y	Medicare	Y	Y	Y
	Inter-mediate		——	—— Mos.	N	Medicaid	N	N	N

| Nursing home | (g) Initial deposit/ down payment | (h) Monthly room charges | | (1) Additional Monthly Services and Charges | | | | | | | | | Esti-mated total monthly charges |
		(1) Private	(2) Semi-private	(1)	(2)	(3)	(4)	(5)	(6)	(7)	(8)	(9)	
	$ ___	$ ___	$ ___	$ ___	$ ___	$ ___	$ ___	$ ___	$ ___	$ ___	$ ___	$ ___	$ ___
	$ ___	$ ___	$ ___	$ ___	$ ___	$ ___	$ ___	$ ___	$ ___	$ ___	$ ___	$ ___	$ ___
	$ ___	$ ___	$ ___	$ ___	$ ___	$ ___	$ ___	$ ___	$ ___	$ ___	$ ___	$ ___	$ ___
	$ ___	$ ___	$ ___	$ ___	$ ___	$ ___	$ ___	$ ___	$ ___	$ ___	$ ___	$ ___	$ ___

Appendix C

National Organizations Concerned with Housing for Older Americans

National Organizations Concerned with Housing for Older Americans

American Association of Retired
Persons (AARP)
1909 K Street
Washington, DC 20049

Center for Community Change
1000 Wisconsin Avenue, NW
Washington, DC 20007

Council of State Housing Agencies
444 North Capitol Street, NW
Suite 118
Washington, DC 20001

Gray Panthers National Office
311 South Juniper Street, Suite 601
Philadelphia, PA 19107

National Association of
Area Agencies on Aging
600 Maryland Avenue, SW
Washington, DC 20024

National Association of
Neighborhoods (NAN)
1651 Fuller Street, NW
Washington, DC 20009

National Association of
State Units on Aging
600 Maryland Avenue, SW
Suite 208
Washington, DC 20024

The National Association of
Retired Federal Employees
1533 New Hampshire Avenue, NW
Washington, DC 20036

The National Caucus and
Center on Black Aged, Inc. (NCBA)
1424 K Street, NW
Suite 500
Washington, DC 20005

National Council of
Senior Citizens
925 15th Street, NW
Washington, DC 20005

The National Council on Aging
600 Maryland Avenue, SW
West Wing 100
Washington, DC 20024

Partners for Livable Places
1429 21st Street, NW
Washington, DC 20036

Appendix D

State Offices on Aging

ALABAMA
Commission on Aging
502 Washington Avenue 2nd Floor
Montgomery, AL 36130
(205) 261-5743

ALASKA
Older Alaskans Commission
Department of Administration
Pouch C-MS-0209
Juneau, AK 99811
(907) 465-3250

ARIZONA
Office on Aging and
Adult Administration
P.O. Box 6123
1400 West Washington Street
Phoenix, AZ 85007
(602) 255-4446

ARKANSAS
Office of Aging and Adult Services
1428 Donaghey Building
7th and Main Streets
Little Rock, AR 72201
(501) 371-2441

CALIFORNIA
Department on Aging, Health
and Welfare
1020 19th Street
Sacramento, CA 95814
(916) 322-5290

COLORADO
Department of Aging and
Adult Services
1575 Sherman Street Room 803
Denver, CO 80203
(303) 866-2586

CONNECTICUT
Department on Aging
175 Main Street
Hartford, CT 06106
(203) 566-7728

DELAWARE
Department of Health and
Social Services
Division on Aging
1901 North Dupont Highway
New Castle, DE 19720
(302) 421-6791

DISTRICT OF COLUMBIA
Office on Aging
1424 K Street, NW 2nd Floor
Washington, DC 20005
(202) 724-5626

FLORIDA
Aging and Adult Services
Department of Health
and Rehabilitative Services
1317 Winewood Boulevard
Tallahassee, FL 32301
(904) 488-8922

GEORGIA
Office on Aging
Department of Human Resources
878 Peachtree Street N.E. Suite 632
Atlanta, GA 30309
(404) 894-5333

HAWAII
Executive Office on Aging
Office of the Governor Room 307
State of Hawaii
1149 Bethel Street
Honolulu, HI 96813
(808) 548-2593

IDAHO
Office on Aging
Statehouse Room 114
Boise, ID 83720
(208) 334-3833

ILLINOIS
Department on Aging
421 East Capitol Avenue
Springfield, IL 62701
(217) 785-3356

INDIANA
Department on Aging and
Community Services Suite 1350
115 North Penn Street
Indianapolis, IN 46204
(317) 232-7006

IOWA
Commission on Aging
236 Jewett Building
Des Moines, IA 50309
(515) 281-5187

KANSAS
Department on Aging
Forbes Credit Union Building
610 West 10th Street
Topeka, KS 66612
(913) 296-4986

KENTUCKY
Division for Aging Services
Department of Social Services
275 East Main Street 6th Floor West
Frankfort, KY 40621
(502) 564-6930

LOUISIANA
Office of Elderly Affairs
P.O. Box 80374
Baton Rouge, LA 70898
(504) 925-1700

MAINE
Bureau of Maine's Elderly
Department of Human Services
State House Station 11
Augusta, ME 04333
(207) 289-2561

MARYLAND
Office on Aging
301 West Preston Street Room 1004
Baltimore, MD 21201
(301) 225-1100

MASSACHUSETTS
Department of Elder Affairs
38 Chauncey Street
Boston, MA 02111
(617) 727-8931

MICHIGAN
Office of Services to the Aging
P.O. Box 30026
Lansing, MI 48909
(517) 373-8230

MINNESOTA
Board on Aging
204 Metro Square Building
121 East 7th Street
St. Paul, MN 55101
(612) 296-2770

MISSISSIPPI
Council on Aging
301 West Pearl Street
Jackson, MS 39203
(601) 949-2070

MISSOURI
Office of Aging
Department of Social Services
505 Missouri Boulevard
P.O. Box 1337
Jefferson City, MO 65102
(314) 751-3082

MONTANA
Community Services Division
Department of Social and
Rehabilitation Services
P.O. Box 4210
Helena, MT 59604
(406) 444-3865

NEBRASKA
Department on Aging
301 Centennial Mall South
Lincoln, NE 68509
(402) 471-2308

NEVADA
Division of Aging Services
Department of Human Resources
505 East King Street
Kinkead Building
Carson City, NV 89710
(702) 855-4210

NEW HAMPSHIRE
Council on the Aging
Prescott Park
105 Loudon Road, Building
3/3rd Fl.
Concord, NH 03301
(603) 271-2751

NEW JERSEY
Department of Community Affairs
363 West State Street
Trenton, NJ 08625
(609) 292-4833

NEW MEXICO
State Agency on Aging
La Villa Rivera Building
224 East Palace Avenue
Santa Fe, NM 87501
(505) 827-7640

NEW YORK
Office for the Aging
Agency Building #2
Empire State Plaza
Albany, NY 12223
(518) 474-5731

NORTH CAROLINA
Division on Aging
Department of Human Resources
708 Hillsborough Street Suite 200
Raleigh, NC 27603
(919) 733-3983

NORTH DAKOTA
Division of Aging Services
State Capitol
Bismark, ND 58505
(701) 224-2577

OHIO
Department of Aging
50 West Broad Street 9th Floor
Columbus, OH 43266-0501
(614) 466-5500

OKLAHOMA
Special Unit on Aging
Department of Human Services
P.O. Box 25352
Oklahoma City, OK 73125
(405) 521-2281

OREGON
Senior Services Division
Human Resources Department
313 Public Services Building
Salem, OR 97301
(503) 378-4728

PENNSYLVANIA
Department of Aging
231 State Street
Harrisburg, PA 17101
(717) 783-1550

RHODE ISLAND
Department of Elderly Affairs
79 Washington Street
Providence, RI 02903
(401) 277-2880

SOUTH CAROLINA
Commission on Aging
915 Main Street
Columbia, SC 29201
(803) 758-2576

SOUTH DAKOTA
Office of Adult Services and Aging
Department of Social Services
701 North Illinois Street
Pierre, SD 57501
(605) 773-3656

TENNESSEE
Commission on Aging
703 Tennessee Building
535 Church Street
Nashville, TN 37219
(615) 741-2056

TEXAS
Department of Aging
P.O. Box 12786
Capitol Station
Austin, Texas 78711
(512) 475-2717

UTAH
Division of Aging Services
P.O. Box 45500
150 West North Temple Street
Salt Lake City, UT 84145
(801) 533-6422

VERMONT
Office on the Aging
103 South Main Street
Waterbury, VT 05676
(802) 241-2400

VIRGINIA
Office on Aging
James Monroe Building
101 North 14th Street 18th Floor
Richmond, VA 23219
(804) 225-2271

WASHINGTON
Bureau of Aging and Adult Services
Department of Social and Health
Services/OB-43G
Olympia, WA 98504
(206) 753-2502

WEST VIRGINIA
Commission on Aging
State Capitol
Charleston, WVA 25305
(304) 348-3317

WISCONSIN
Department of Health
and Social Services
1 West Wilson Street Room 480
Madison, WI 53702
(608-266-2536

WYOMING
Commission on Aging
Hathaway Building, Room 139
Cheyenne, WY 82002
(307) 777-7986

Appendix E

Nursing Home Ombudsman Offices

ALABAMA
Commission on Aging
502 Washington Avenue 2nd Floor
Montgomery, AL 36130
(205) 261-5743

ALASKA
Long-Term Care Ombudsman Office
1317 West Northern Lights, Suite 9
Anchorage, AK 99503
(907) 279-2232

ARIZONA
Long-Term Care Ombudsman Office
Office of Aging and Adult
Administration
1400 West Washington Street/950A
Phoenix, AZ 85007
(602) 255-4446

ARKANSAS
Office on Aging and Adult
Department of Human Services
Donaghey Building
7th and Main Street
Little Rock, AR 72201
(501) 371-2441

CALIFORNIA
Long-Term Care Ombudsman
1020 19th Street
Sacramento, CA 95814
(916) 322-3887

COLORADO
Long-Term Care Ombudsman Office
1565 Clarkson Street
Denver, CO 80218
(303) 837-8285

CONNECTICUT
Department on Aging
175 Main Street
Hartford, CT 06106
(203) 566-7770

DELAWARE
Long-Term Care Ombudsman Office
507 West 9th Street
Wilmington, DE 19801
(302) 655-3451

DISTRICT OF COLUMBIA
Office on Aging
1424 K Street, NW, 2nd Floor
Washington, DC 20005
(202) 724-5622

FLORIDA
Office of Aging and Adult Services
Department of Health and
Rehabilitative Services
1317 Winewood Boulevard
Tallahassee, FL 32301
(904) 488-2650

GEORGIA
Office on Aging
Department of Human Resources
878 Peachtree Street, NE
Suite 642
Atlanta, GA 30309
(404) 894-5336

HAWAII
Executive Office on Aging
Office of the Governer
1149 Bethel Street Room 307
Honolulu, HI 96813
(808) 548-2593

IDAHO
Office on Aging
Statehouse Room 114
Boise, ID 83720
(208) 334-3833

ILLINOIS
Department on Aging
421 East Capitol Avenue
Springfield, IL 62701
(217) 785-0152

INDIANA
Long-Term Care Ombudsman Office
107 North Pennsylvania Avenue
Suite 300, 3rd Floor
Indianapolis, IN 46204
(317) 634-6122

IOWA
Commission on Aging
236 Jewett Building
914 Grand Street
Des Moines, IA 50309
(515) 281-5187

KANSAS
Department on Aging/Ombudsman Off.
610 West 10th Street
Topeka, KS 66612
(913) 296-4986

KENTUCKY
Long-Term Care Ombudsman Office
Department for Human Resources
275 East Main Street
Frankfort, KY 40621
(502) 564-5498

LOUISIANA
Long-Term Care Ombudsman Office
Bureau of Aging Services
Department of Health and
Human Resources
P.O. Box 44282, Capitol Station
Baton Rouge, LA 70804
(504) 342-2756

MAINE
Long-Term Care Ombudsman Office
Maine Committee on Aging
State House Station 11
Augusta, ME 04333
(207) 289-3658

MARYLAND
Long-Term Care Ombudsman Office
Office on Aging
301 West Preston Street Room 1004
Baltimore, MD 21201
(301) 225-1083

MASSACHUSETTS
Executive Office of Elder Affairs
38 Chauncey Street
Boston, MA 02111
(617) 727-7273

MICHIGAN
Long-Term Care Ombudsman Office
Citizens for Better Care
900 West Ottawa Street
Lansing, MI 48915
(517) 482-1297

MINNESOTA
Long-Term Care Ombudsman Office
Board on Aging
204 Metro Square Building
121 East 7th Street
St. Paul, MN 55101
(612) 296-2770

MISSISSIPPI
Long-Term Care Ombudsman Office
Council on Aging
301 West Pearl Street
Jackson, MS 32903
(601) 354-7011

MISSOURI
Long-Term Care Ombudsman Office
Division on Aging
505 Missouri Boulevard[/]P.O.Box 1337
Jefferson City, MO 65101
(314) 751-3082

MONTANA
Long-Term Care Ombudsman Office
P.O. Box 232
Capitol Station
Helena, MT 59620
(406) 444-4676

NEBRASKA
Long-Term Care Ombudsman Office
Department on Aging
State House Station Box 95044
Lincoln, NE 68509
(402) 471-2307

NEVADA
Long-Term Care Ombudsman Office
Division on Aging
Department of Human Resources
505 East King Street
Kinkead Building, Room 101
Carson City, NV 89710
(702) 885-4210

NEW HAMPSHIRE
State Long-Term Care
Ombudsman Office
105 Loudon Road, Building, 3
Concord, NH 03301
(603) 271-2751

NEW JERSEY
Office of the Ombudsman for the
Institutionalized Elderly
28 West State Street CN 808
Trenton, NJ 08625
(609) 292-8016

NEW MEXICO
State Ombudsman Office
State Agency on Aging
La Villa Rivera Building
224 East Palace Avenue
Santa Fe, NM 87501
(505) 827-7640

NEW YORK
(State Office for the Aging
Agency Building #2)
Empire State Plaza
Albany, NY 12223
(518) 474-7329

NORTH CAROLINA
State Long-Term Care
Ombudsman Office
708 Hillsborough Street Suite 200
Raleigh, NC 27603
(919) 733-3983

NORTH DAKOTA
Long-Term Care Ombudsman Office
Division of Aging Services
State Capitol
Bismarck, ND 58505
(701) 224-2577

OHIO
Long-Term Care Ombudsman Office
Commission on Aging
50 West Broad Street 9th Floor
Columbus, OH 43266
(614) 466-1220

OKLAHOMA
Long-Term Care Ombudsman Office
Special Unit on Aging
P.O. Box 25352
Oklahoma City, OK 73125
(405) 521-2281

OREGON
Long-Term Care Ombudsman Office
160 State Capitol
Salem, OR 97310
(503) 378-6533

PENNSYLVANIA
Long-Term Care Ombudsman Office
231 State Street/Barto Building
Harrisburg, PA 17101
(717) 783-7247

RHODE ISLAND
Long-Term Care Ombudsman Office
Department of Elderly Affairs
79 Washington Street
Providence, RI 02903
(401) 277-6880

SOUTH CAROLINA
Long-Term Care Ombudsman Office
1205 Pendletown Street Room 412
Columbia, SC 29201
(803) 758-2249

SOUTH DAKOTA
Department of Social Services
Office of Adult Services and Aging
700 North Illinois Street
Pierre, SD 57501
(605) 773-3656

TENNESSEE
Commission on Aging
703 Tennessee Building
535 Church Street
Nashville, TN 37219
(615) 741-2056

TEXAS
Department on Aging
P.O. Box 12786
Capitol Station
Austin, TX 78711
(512) 475-2717

UTAH
State Ombudsman Office
Division of Aging Services
150 West North Temple Street
Salt Lake City, UT 84145
(801) 533-6422

VERMONT
Office on Aging
103 South Main Street
Waterbury, VT 05676
(802) 241-2400

VIRGINIA
Office on Aging
James Monroe Building
101 North 14th Street 18th Floor
Richmond, VA 23219
(804) 225-2271

WASHINGTON
Long-Term Care Ombudsman Office
Department of Social and Health
Services/OB33-B
Olympia, WA 98504
(206) 754-2258

WEST VIRGINIA
Long-Term Care Ombudsman Office
Commission on Aging
State Capitol
Charleston, WVA 25305
(304) 348-2243

WISCONSIN
Board on Aging and Long-Term Care
819 North 6th Street, Room 619
Milwaukee, WI 53203
(414) 224-4386

WYOMING
Long-Term Care Ombudsman Office
814 8th Street
Wheatland, WY 82201
(307) 322-5553

Index